Advertising
Media Planning

Advertising
Media Planning
A Brand Management Approach

Second Edition

Larry D. Kelley and Donald W. Jugenheimer

M.E.Sharpe
Armonk, New York
London, England

Library of Congress Cataloging-in-Publication Data

Kelley, Larry D., 1955–
   Advertising media planning : a brand management approach / by Larry D. Kelley and
Donald W. Jugenheimer. — 2nd ed.
      p. cm.
   Includes index.
   ISBN 978-0-7656-2032-3 (cloth : alk. paper)— ISBN 978-0-7656-2033-0 (pbk. : alk. paper)
   1. Advertising media planning. 2. Brand name products. 3. Marketing. I. Jugenheimer,
Donald W. II. Title.

HF5826.5.K45 2008
659.1′11—dc22

2007022346

Printed in the United States of America

BM (c)   10   9   8   7   6   5   4   3   2   1
BM (p)   10   9   8   7   6   5   4   3

Contents

Preface

This is the second edition of *Advertising Media Planning: A Brand Management Approach,* a book that can be used by anyone making advertising and promotional media decisions. Media planning is a crucial part of the advertising process—and ultimately of the brand management process—yet little has been written on how brand management can impact the media process. Our goal with the initial edition of this book was to fill that void in the market. Our second edition takes it many steps further, showing the media planning process from the viewpoints of both the media planner and the brand manager. All of the stakeholders of a media plan have input and control over various aspects of its outcome.

The second edition of this book begins by laying the basic foundation of media and then takes you through the steps that impact a media program, explaining how brand decisions are woven into the process. The book subsequently details the making of a media plan, the process of evaluating the plan's effectiveness, and the ultimate media execution resulting from it.

This edition of *Advertising Media Planning* ties into the second edition of *Advertising Media Workbook and Sourcebook,* also published by M.E. Sharpe. For students and instructors of media planning courses, the workbook offers a detailed perspective of each facet of media, along with practical exercises offering students the opportunity to put sometimes abstract concepts into real world situations.

As the world of media has changed, so has our second edition. It contains up-to-date information on the exploding world of interactive media and the changing nature of media planning from an efficiency driven exercise to a consumer engagement process.

Within this ever-changing field of media, there are more reasons than ever to have a "go to" source that any level of media decision maker can use to help make crucial decisions impacting a brand's value. Brand managers who have little formal training in advertising media, students of advertising and integrated marketing communications programs, and other practitioners such as account supervisors and media salespersons can benefit from this book's straightforward, hands-on approach to the business of advertising media.

Acknowledgments

The authors would like to thank the following persons for their help and support during the writing and editing of this book: Debbie Thompson Stanford, who worked diligently on getting the manuscript in its final form; Harry Briggs, our editor and publisher; and Elizabeth Granda, who helped us negotiate the production cycle. We especially want to thank our spouses and families for all their support, without which this project would not have been possible.

Advertising
Media Planning

Chapter 1

Why Media Are Important

You are a brand manager. You are responsible for the marketing success of a product or service, or a brand, or maybe an entire line of goods. Your personal and professional success depends on your brand's success. Perhaps you are an advertising account executive or account supervisor, or even a top-level executive who wants the entire company or corporation to do well. The success of your advertising is crucial to your product's welfare and success.

Whatever your job title, you are concerned with the sale of the product or service that you are marketing. Sure, you are interested in the advertising campaign strategy, and you review and approve all the advertising copy and themes before they go to production. However, the media portion of the campaign may not really interest you. After all, it is detailed, it is somewhat abstract, and it is invariably complicated. You may believe that the heart of advertising is the message, so you probably concentrate on the theme, headlines, visuals, and copy. You may give cursory review to the research and to the media plan, but they are not your primary focus. Or maybe you do not delve deeply into the media plan because you do not fully understand the concepts and workings of advertising media.

So why should you be so interested in advertising media and the media plans that underscore your campaign? There are several reasons why advertising media are important to you and critical to the success of your advertising.

Media: Most of the Budget

First, advertising media take up most of the advertising budget. Media time and space are expensive: in a typical advertising campaign, the media costs account for 80 to 85 percent of the advertising budget; the remaining 15 or 20 percent covers research, message, production, evaluation, and profits for the advertising agency (See Exhibit 1.1).

If advertising media control the bulk of your advertising budget, you should spend sufficient time and effort making sure that the media plans are sensible and that the media selection and purchases are relevant and efficient.

Exhibit 1.1

Typical Allocations for a Consumer Advertising Campaign

A typical advertising campaign budget is divided up for a variety of needs and purposes. Here is a sample advertising budget from a campaign to promote a consumer packaged good.

Budget item	Budget allocation (%)
Research, precampaign, and postcampaign evaluation	3–6
Message development	5–8
Advertising media	80–85
Production	4–7
Overhead, administration, agency profits	1–3

Source: Advertising Research Foundation, 2002.

In most situations, 20 percent of the efforts produce 80 percent of the revenue. You may be spending only 20 percent of your effort on the 80 percent of the advertising campaign that will make or break your campaign success. Anything that accounts for 80 percent of the monies and a large share of the campaign success deserves a great share of your attention and effort.

Advertising media may seem complicated and somewhat arcane to you. The purpose of this book is to give you the background and information you need to be an informed and capable manager, one who understands and administers the entire advertising effort, including the media planning, selection, and buying.

So advertising media account for most of your advertising budget and are therefore worthy of your attention and interest. But there are more reasons why advertising media are important to you.

A Poor Media Plan Sabotages an Entire Campaign

Let's say you have a great advertising campaign plan. The theme is memorable, the visuals are impressive, and the words are emphatic. What good is it if those message elements do not reach the intended audience?

Suppose you're selling canned soup. The media team targets traditional users of canned soup—mothers of young children—but the copy team prepares advertisements intended to encourage single people to use the soup for a quick, wholesome meal. The message will not make much sense to the media audience because the media and copy strategies do not match.

A great advertising message in front of the wrong audience is a total waste of time and effort. If you focus on the message strategies and ignore the media strategies, you risk sabotaging the entire package: the campaign, the budget, and everyone's hard work.

That, of course, is where the advertising media plan plays its role. A solid media plan with good media selection and media buying can ensure that the message reaches the right people at the right time and in the right mood. Based on solid research, a good media effort is what makes the rest of the advertising campaign work—or not work.

Media Are Least Understood

Most advertising campaigns are sold to the client advertiser on the basis of the message. If the message is good, the campaign is more likely to be adopted. That's because the message is inherently the most interesting part of the advertising campaign. And it should be: the message is what is going to attract, inform, entertain, promote, convince, and sell your service or product. It is supposed to be attractive and interesting.

The advertising agency stresses the message, the advertiser client sees and hears the message, and the prospective campaign is adopted largely on the basis of the message. Typically, the advertiser or client pays attention to messages and promotions, and maybe even to research, but not to the media plan. To match the clients' interests in a proposed advertising campaign, the advertising agency presents more material dealing with the message and not as much with research, production, evaluation, or media.

So most proposed campaign presentations spend the most time on the message strategies and relatively little on the media portion of the campaign. The top executives may assume that the media plan is complete and logical, but that is not always the case.

This is precisely why you need to pay attention to the media plan. If others tend to understress it or overlook it, you are the one responsible for making sure that the media plan makes sense and can be accomplished efficiently and accurately for the total success of the advertising campaign.

Media Are Critical to Success of the Brand

Obviously, then, advertising media are critical to advertising success. Advertising success brings with it the achievement of the marketing goals: more sales, positive opinions, increased awareness, word-of-mouth recommendations, competitive advantages, or whatever your goals may happen to be. Accomplishing those goals makes your brand successful, and hanging on that brand success is your success as a brand manager, or as an account executive or supervisor or administrator.

Advertising media are critical to the success of the brand and thus critical to your success as a manager. As we have already seen, poor media choices can waste an entire advertising campaign. On the other hand, proper and efficient use of advertising media can underwrite the success of an entire campaign. It is up to you to be certain that the media contribute all they potentially can to help you make your brand a success.

Client Exposure to the Advertising

Advertisers like to see their own advertising. Top executives know how much is being spent on advertising, and they want to see and hear that advertising in the media. Those top executives who know and approve total advertising budgets are not likely to understand the nuances of advertising, including advertising media. They simply know that they are spending large sums of money to promote their products and services, and they want to see effective outcomes. These outcomes may eventually be product sales and brand preference, but in the meantime, executives simply want to see their advertising running in the media.

You may not target media specifically to reach those executives. You may not even know which media the executives listen to or watch. Yet, if your media plan reaches your industry and your prospects, you should be reaching your own executives and supervisors as well.

Good media plans make sure that the advertisements appear in places where they will be exposed to your firm's executives. The only way to be certain that will happen is if you are on top of advertising media in general, and your specific advertising media plan in particular.

Media Support Product Positioning

Perhaps the most crucial decisions you make involve positioning for the product or service that you are marketing. Brand positioning plays a critical role in the success or failure of your marketing program. Once the position has been determined, it must be translated into advertising; the positioning is meaningless if it is not supported in the advertising.

One of the most sensible and direct ways of translating positioning into advertising is through advertising media. The media reach those same customers whom you have selected as the target audience for the brand and its position. There is no way that positioning will be successful if it is not supported adequately and accurately through the media selections and placements.

So successful marketing depends on successful positioning. If you want your positioning to be successful, you must select and utilize advertising media effectively, efficiently, and, above all, accurately. Advertising media play an essential role in your brand's success and, ultimately, in your own success and progress.

The Ever-Changing World of Media

The basics of good marketing communications have remained fairly constant over the years, and positioning strategy has changed only slightly since the late 1980s. However, advertising media have evolved rapidly over the past 10 years, led principally by the digital media revolution.

We have certainly seen the rise of new kinds of advertising media over the past decade. The Internet has led the way with a wide variety of media such as search engine marketing, rich media, and streaming audio and video. Other media channels have come into play, including the iPod, cellular phones, video games, and satellite radio. Existing media have evolved as well. The area of point-of-sale advertising has been transformed in the twenty-first century, with opportunities appearing in seemingly every venue. Malls now have digital signs that show television commercials. In some major markets, buses contain television sets that are programmed to show a retail ad within a block or two of the advertising establishment. Ads are popping up in elevators, inside fortune cookies, and even on celebrity and "wanna-be" celebrity body parts.

The rise of consumer-generated media is redefining the media landscape as well. Now, anyone with a video camera can shoot a commercial and post it on the Internet. Blogs, which are personal journals posted on the Net, allow everyone the freedom to comment on whatever they want. Fundamentally, anything can become a medium these days for good or bad.

This digital revolution has changed the way that advertisers and marketers approach media. Before the digital revolution, advertising pushed a message out to consumers with little direct feedback. Today, consumers are providing feedback to marketers through their own media and by asking for deals from selective advertisers. This type of marketing is a dialogue-based rather than push-based messaging.

The advertising industry has also undergone major structural changes. At one time, media ownership was largely a "mom and pop" business. Individual families owned a local newspaper, radio station, or television station. Today, there has been massive consolidation of media outlets. There were once hundreds of radio station owners, and at one time Clear Channel owned more than half of all radio stations in the United States. Time Warner controls a host of mass and interpersonal media, from magazines to television to Internet to motion pictures. Within the past 10 years, the power of search engine marketing companies such as Google has brought a new wave of corporations to what used to be a very clubby business.

The jury is still out on the social and marketing impact of this media ownership consolidation. Many people fear that news and information are stilted by being controlled by a few companies. To counter that argument, we have seen the rise of consumer-generated media as a collective voice in many social circumstances. From a marketing viewpoint, advertisers feared that media mergers would bring higher advertising rates. However, with so many new media on the horizon, this has also become a moot point. What we are seeing is the rise of multimedia companies providing content for advertisers that crosses a variety of platforms.

The Changing Nature of Media Effectiveness

Media plans and media buys have long been judged on their efficiency, but new emphasis is being given to how consumers use media, how media impact the creative content, and when consumers are most susceptible to the message.

Let's tackle the area of susceptibility first. Psychologists have long debated whether primacy or recency is more important in advertising. Does it help more to be the first advertisement seen or heard in your product category, or is it better to be the last advertisement seen or heard before the consumer makes a purchase decision? The current trend in advertising is for recency, which affects both the frequency and placement of advertising. For example, if you know that most consumers make a meal decision an hour or two before they eat, then you may want to load up your advertising to intercept them at that moment. Looking at the media world through the consumers' eyes is an evolving area in media studies. Media planners have traditionally used syndicated research to determine what consumers watched, read, or listened to and then crafted media plans that were the most efficient combination of those elements. Today, media planners continue to look at syndicated data, but they are more likely to conduct their own consumer research. They may observe how consumers use media or how various media influence their decisions about a brand. For example, a recent study showed marked differences in consumers' views of media for impulse items versus planned purchases. So, effectiveness in this case might be to find the media that fit best with an impulse purchase decision. This type of thinking is much more in line with consumer behavior theory than media theory and has led to a number of studies regarding the role of media in the creative message. For example, if a brand's success is based on a high degree of trust, would you be better off placing it on the nightly news or in a soap opera? This study found that there is a significant copy recall benefit for the brand to be in the nightly news versus the soap opera. Media effectiveness is certainly an evolving aspect of the media landscape.

Media are also looked at in a return-on-investment perspective. In fact, media are sales channels for many brands. Retailers may have stores, Web site sales, catalogs, and kiosks. They may know exactly what a particular Sunday insert does for their business. Most service brands track the source of their leads, whether they are through the Yellow Pages or local search engine marketing or word of mouth. Brand marketers conduct rigorous analyses to determine the lift that each medium and vehicle gives to incremental brand sales. And business-to-business brand managers are using media to sell merchandise directly. The PC company Dell is a prime example of this type of advertising, where each sale is coded to a particular media and message source.

All these recent changes and future developments make it mandatory that everyone who works with advertising—and especially brand managers—has a working knowledge of how advertising media operate and the role they play in the overall advertising and marketing efforts.

Good Media Planning Increases Efficiency

As we have said, media efficiency is a primary goal of advertising media planning and buying. Efficiency, though, does not always mean getting the lowest price. In this case, we look at efficiency in terms of having the optimum amount of advertising to do the job. No firm wants to waste money, and that includes not wasting the advertising budget.

Too much media overlap is inefficient. If the selected media and vehicles all reach the same audience, advertisers risk losing out on a broader audience that can help build market breadth.

Too much frequency is also inefficient. You want to advertise enough so that your customers do what you want them to do: switch brands, think favorably of your brand, know your product's attributes, or simply buy your product. You want your advertising to reach them enough times to accomplish those goals. More than that may be unnecessary.

Too many nonprospects seeing your advertising is inefficient, too. Your advertising should reach genuine prospects. Advertising that does not focus on those who are genuine prospects is wasteful.

A solid advertising media plan can avoid the inefficiencies of excessive overlap, frequency, and waste. Certainly, some media overlap is desirable to reinforce the message in a variety of ways and from a variety of sources. Frequency of exposure is also important: seeing or hearing your advertising message only once is unlikely to work. Similarly, it is impossible to reach all your prospects and only your prospects; some coverage will go to nonprospects. A golf equipment campaign that uses both *Golf Digest* and *Sports Illustrated* will find that some audience members read both publications; that is not necessarily bad, but make sure that you count the double exposure in your calculations of total audience impressions to minimize the possibility of wasteful overlap. For a bread account, an average exposure level of 20 times a week is probably excessive; frequency is important, but overdoing it wastes money. If you sell dog food, it may not be possible to reach dog owners and only dog owners; still, you do not want much of your advertising to appear before those who do not have dogs and are not likely buying your dog food. Knowledge of advertising media and media planning will help you avoid these excessive and wasteful practices, which will lead to yet another benefit.

Media Efficiency Provides Budget Flexibility

If you reduce waste, you save money. Saving money means that your budget will go further, you will have money left over for other uses, and you can afford to underwrite additional promotions.

Your knowledge and understanding of advertising media planning can help you avoid the excesses of overlap, frequency, and waste, achieving the correct levels of exposure without going beyond them. In turn, you will then have more money left in your budget. Leftover monies mean greater flexibility; more advertising and promotions; increased product awareness, knowledge, and sales; and quicker and greater brand success. And those are your goals. Efficiency in your use of advertising media helps you have more funds to achieve all your goals, making you and your brand successful.

If your automotive service campaign reduces excessive media overlap, cuts frequency of advertising closer to the minimal effective level, and avoids reaching audiences who do not own cars, you may be able to save enough money from your advertising budget to run additional promotions, to introduce a new add-on service, to promote dollars-off or coupon offers, or perhaps to start a special selling effort aimed at getting competitors' customers to switch to your service. These new additions are certain to increase your chances of higher sales and more revenue.

Gaining efficiency makes sense, whether to save money or to provide remainder funds for new efforts. To use advertising media efficiently and to understand advertising media planning, it is necessary to comprehend the language of advertising media, which is the focus of the next chapter.

Chapter 2

Learning the Language of Media

To understand how any business operates, you must know the language of that business. It is the same in advertising: when you know the terminology of advertising media, you will be well on your way to understanding the process and function of the mass media in your advertising campaign.

Knowing terminology can do even more. By knowing the terms and concepts of advertising media, you can contribute your own ideas and precepts, you can envision how the entire advertising campaign fits together, and you can be accepted as a knowledgeable, contributing partner in the campaign development process.

Advertising media terminology is not difficult or complicated. Nobody tried to create complicated terms to describe how the media work. Instead, the terminology just developed along with the industry, so many of the terms make logical sense in how they are defined and used. But at the same time, nobody wants to stop in the middle of a discussion to define terms for you; everyone assumes that you know the terminology. You must know these terms as well as you know other basic concepts, like "right" or "left," "up" or "down." You will not have time to stop and figure out the terms in the middle of a meeting; work and ideas move rapidly in advertising, so the terminology must be second nature to you.

Here, then, in simple and direct language, are the basic terms used in advertising media planning.

We can start with the term *media.* The *media* are go-betweens, the facilitators that make it possible to deliver an advertising message. The term *media* is plural; the singular is *medium.* The alternate plural, *mediums,* refers to fortune-tellers and seers, not advertising. A single media outlet, such as a magazine, a broadcast network, a radio station, or a newspaper, is called a *media vehicle.* The specifications of the individual advertisement are the *advertising unit.* For example, if your media choice is magazines, your vehicle might be *Family Circle,* and your advertising unit might be a full-page, four-color bleed advertisement.

The Four Basics

There are four basic concepts that underlie most advertising: *reach, frequency, impact,* and *continuity.* Be sure to master these four basic terms because they are used commonly and serve as a foundation for much of what happens in advertising media planning.

Reach

There are two kinds of reach: *numerical* and *percentage.* Numerical reach is the number of persons (or households, or adult females, or whatever your target population happens to be) to whom your advertising will be communicated. Numerical reach is usually rounded, so you may try to reach 8 million male teens or 1.5 million households.

Percentage reach is the percent of all the persons (or, again, households, or working females, or whatever your target) that you will reach with your campaign. If there are 35 million college students in the United States and you will reach 10 million of them, you will reach about 28.6 percent of them. Because percentage reach is often rounded to the nearest integer (whole number), you would have 29 percent reach in this case.

Reach is often abbreviated as "R" in tables and informal reports.

Frequency

There are also two kinds of frequency: *frequency of insertion* and *frequency of exposure.*

Frequency of insertion describes the number of times that your advertisement appears in the media. Often, frequency is described on a per-week basis, rather than the frequency per year or the frequency during the course of a campaign. So you might be running your advertising 25 times per week on a radio station during your 13-week campaign.

Just because you run advertising insertions frequently does not mean that the audience will see or hear your advertisement every time it runs. In fact, it is unlikely that *any* member of your audience will be exposed to your advertising every time it runs. If you have a frequency of insertion of 25 times per week, the average audience member will see or hear that advertisement only three or four times each week, which would be your frequency of exposure.

When scheduling multiple advertisement insertions, you are likely to reach your audience members with varying degrees of frequency. If you schedule, say, 10 advertisements, perhaps only 10 percent of the audience

Exhibit 2.1

Frequency and Repetition

Some people believe that frequency and repetition are the same thing, but they are not. Frequency is the number of times you advertise, whether the same message is repeated or not. Repetition is using the same advertising message over and over again, whether it is done frequently or not.

A local store buys 25 spots per week on a local radio station and has the messages delivered impromptu by one of the station's on-air personalities. The advertising is appearing frequently, but it is unlikely that any of the messages is repeated exactly. Here we have frequency without repetition.

A large insurance company runs its Christmas message in magazines every December, using the same message every year. Advertising one time per year is definitely not frequent advertising, so here we have repetition without frequency.

members will see all 10 and 30 percent will see only one. One method that a media planner uses to analyze the impact of an advertising media schedule is to look at a frequency distribution of the impressions.

There are different schools of thought on how many times consumers must see or hear an advertisement before it registers in their minds. The concept of effective frequency pegs a specific frequency number, such as 3+ (persons who see or hear the advertisement three or more times), which is when it is believed that a consumer will retain the message.

Frequency is often abbreviated as "F" in informal plans and tables. Because no single week may be completely representative or average, we often count up the frequency over a four-week period and then divide the figure by four to come up with the weekly average. That way, a week that is higher or lower than average will not skew the figures.

Impact

The *impact* that an advertisement has on the audience is the result of a number of factors, many of them relating to the message: headline, illustration, body copy, and other message components. The media contribution to impact comes from the size of a print advertisement or the length of a broadcast commercial or from the use of color or bleed (print that appears to "bleed" off the edge of the page) or reverse (e.g., white type on black background) printing. These advertising unit specifications, then, define the impact that is derived from the media portion of the campaign.

Continuity

Continuity involves the scheduling of the advertisement. You want to plan the pattern of your advertising so that subsequent messages build on top of the gains made by previous insertions. If the advertisements are scheduled too far apart, you may be starting over with each new ad because the audience has forgotten what you said in previous advertisements. On the other hand, if you schedule your advertising properly, each subsequent ad will appear before the effects have worn off from previous advertising, so you gain a cumulative effect. Proper scheduling can provide continuity. Continuity is the pattern of advertising, with messages scheduled for maximum effect.

Buying more reach in advertising costs more money. Similarly, buying more frequency costs more money. And buying more impact (larger advertisements, longer commercials, color, etc.) costs more money. Continuity, on the other hand, does not necessarily cost more money; it involves scheduling the optimal pattern of advertising, not necessarily buying more advertising.

Audience Measures

Copies Printed vs. People in the Audience

Different media accumulate their audiences in different ways. In print media, such as newspapers and magazines, the first part of the statistic is the actual number of publications distributed, or circulation. However, more than one person usually reads each copy of a publication; for example, most newspapers average two readers per copy, while certain magazines, such as *People,* may have upwards of eight readers per copy. So the total audience is the circulation multiplied by the readers per copy. Thus, in print media, such as newspapers and magazines, the circulation is the number of copies printed, while the audience is the number of persons who read those copies of the publication. Because you want to attract more than one reader per copy of the publication, the number for the audience will usually be larger than the number for circulation.

Table 2.1

Accumulative Audience

Insertion #	New readers	
1	500,000	
2	100,000	
3	50,000	
	650,000	Total

Note: New readers are those who have not seen the advertising before.

Outdoor advertising also has a circulation measure. Each billboard has a Daily Effective Circulation, or DEC, which is the actual number of people who drive by or see that billboard. To get the total audience, you simply multiply by the number of days that particular poster is showing.

Broadcast media, on the other hand, have no circulation measure. The audience is measured by a random sample of viewers or listeners. The Internet also has no circulation figures but is measured in a similar manner as broadcast, with one single measurement.

Accumulative Audience

As we have just seen, numerical reach measures the size of your audience. But confusion can result between the reach for a single advertising insertion and the total reach for a series of advertisements or for an entire campaign. To reduce this confusion, the term *accumulative audience* (also called *cumulative audience,* or *cume*) is used to refer to the audience of a series of advertising placements or of an advertising campaign. (See Table 2.1.)

If you run a series of advertisements in a single media vehicle, the total number of audience members you have reached is the accumulative audience. For example, let's say you run three advertisements in the *Chicago Tribune.* The accumulative audience is the total number of different people who have been exposed to your campaign in that single media vehicle. Each audience member is counted only once, no matter how many times he or she may have seen the advertising.

Unduplicated Audience

Similarly, if you run your advertising in a combination of vehicles, the total audience size is called the *unduplicated audience.* Again, each audience member is counted only once, no matter how many times he or she may have heard or seen your advertisements; counting a person again would inflate your unduplicated audience figures.

Let's say you are advertising in *Newsweek* magazine and on the *NBC Nightly News.* Whether audience members see your advertising in *Newsweek* or hear it on the nightly news or both, they are each counted only once.

The unduplicated audience is very much like the accumulative audience. The difference is that the accumulative audience involves the total number of different people who are exposed to your advertising through a combination of advertisements in a *single vehicle,* whereas the unduplicated audience is the total number of different people who are exposed to your advertising through a series of advertisements in a *combination of vehicles.* These terms are often misused in the advertising business, particularly by persons who are not knowledgeable or experienced in the media portion of the business. The most common error is for someone to use *unduplicated audience* for both unduplicated and accumulative audiences. Such an error is not a major sin, but keeping the terms straight can help avoid confusion and add efficiency and accuracy to your media planning.

Audience Percentage Measurements

The terms *rating* and *share* are not difficult to understand once you grasp the basic concepts that underlie them. Because they began as broadcast terms, perhaps using broadcast examples will make them easier to comprehend. Although both terms deal with the percentage of audience members who are exposed to your advertising, each percent is calculated as a portion of different populations.

First, it will help to understand what is meant by a television household, abbreviated as TVHH in the media business. A household is a group of people who live together, most often a family, but also a single person living alone, persons of the opposite sex sharing living quarters (what the government abbreviates as POSSLQ), or roommates. A television household is a household that has an operating television set; the set may be on or off, because the term "operating" means that the receiving set works, not that it is being used at any particular moment.

Another common term is Households Using Television, abbreviated as HUT. It refers to the television households with a set turned on as a percentage of all television households. The major radio ratings service reports on People Using Radio, abbreviated as PUR, which is persons listening to the radio expressed as a percentage of all people with radios.

Rating

In television broadcasting, the rating refers to the persons who see or hear a particular program, station, or network expressed as a percentage of all TVHH, whether they have a set on at that moment or not. The rating can be for a certain region or broadcast area, or it can be for the entire country.

Similarly, a radio rating is those persons tuned to a particular program, station, or network expressed as a percentage of all the households that have operating radio receivers, counting all radios, those in use and those turned off at that particular time.

Rating is often abbreviated as "Rtg."

Share

Again using television broadcasting for the example, the share is those persons tuned to a particular program station or network as a percentage of all television households with sets turned on, that is, as a percentage of HUT. The share could be for the entire country or for a particular geographic market. A radio share is those persons tuned in as a percentage of all households that have their radios on at that time (the Households Using Radio, or HUR). Share is often abbreviated as "Shr."

So both rating and share involve the same people, those tuned to a particular program, station, or network at a particular time. Rating is those persons as a percentage of all the households with receiving sets, whether they are on or not at that particular time, and share is those same persons as a percentage of all those with sets on at that moment. (See Exhibit 2.2.)

Let's say that there are 100,000 television households in Erie, Pennsylvania, and that 60,000 of those households have their television sets on at 8 P.M., and that 20,000 of those households are watching a particular station in Erie. The station's rating would be 20 percent and its share would be 33 percent.

$$\text{Rating} = \frac{20,000}{100,000} = 20 \text{ percent} \qquad \text{Share} = \frac{20,000}{60,000} = 33 \text{ percent}$$

Because the concepts of rating and share are so useful, they have been applied to all types of media: print, outdoor, and new media, as well as broadcast media. In print, however, we cannot have a publication turned on or off at a particular time, so instead we usually use the entire population or all the households as the size of the potential audience. A newspaper with a circulation of 25,000 in a market of 100,000 households would have a 25 percent rating. In print media, ratings are commonly discussed as coverage.

Rating is likely to be applied to all the media, because it is a more useful

Exhibit 2.2

An Example of Ratings and Shares

Palookaville has four television stations serving its population of 250,000 television households (TVHH). For 8 P.M. on Wednesdays, when 54,000 TVHH have their sets on, here are the ratings and shares for the four stations.

Television station	TVHH sets on	Rtg	Shr
KAAA	12,000	$\frac{12,000}{250,000} = 4.8$	$\frac{12,000}{54,000} = 22$
KBBB	15,000	$\frac{15,000}{250,000} = 6.0$	$\frac{15,000}{54,000} = 28$
KCCC	18,000	$\frac{18,000}{250,000} = 7.2$	$\frac{18,000}{54,000} = 33$
KDDD	9,000	$\frac{9,000}{250,000} = 3.6$	$\frac{9,000}{54,000} = 17$
		21.6 HUT	100%

$$HUT = \frac{54,000}{250,000} = 21.6\%$$

Note that you can quickly check your calculations by adding the ratings to compare with the HUT that you have calculated.

concept for advertisers than the share is. The share tells how well a media vehicle competes with other vehicles in that marketplace, which is most useful to the broadcaster or publisher. Rating, on the other hand, tells how that time or space segment fares with the total potential audience in that marketplace. These terms are applied to the particular time segment when a commercial runs or the particular print segment where an advertisement appears, so the rating or share for an advertisement concentrates on only that time or place where the advertisement is run.

Combining Reach and Frequency for Audience Totals

Because reach and frequency are so important, it makes sense that a figure combining both reach and frequency would also be useful. In fact, we have two such combination figures.

Gross Rating Points and Target Rating Points

The sum of the ratings for a certain period of time is called the *gross rating points,* abbreviated as GRP. Let's say you are running five advertisements a week on a television network, and the ratings look like this.

Spot #	Rtg (%)
1	11
2	8
3	12
4	10
5	9
Total	50 GRP

But also notice that we have run five spots for a total of 50 GRP, which means the average spot pulled a rating of 10 percent. So 5 is the frequency and 10 is the average rating, or the average percentage reach. Thus, our 50 GRP gave us averages of 10 percent reach or an average rating of 10 combined with the frequency of 5. As you can see, the GRP gives us a combination of reach (10 percent in this example) and frequency (5 in this example) in a single figure.

$$10 \text{ R} \times 5 \text{ F} = 50 \text{ GRP}$$

So *reach* (as a percent) multiplied by *frequency* produces *gross rating points.*

$$\text{R\%} \times \text{F} = \text{GRP}$$

Also keep in mind that a single rating, called a rating point, reaches 1 percent of the audience.

As advertising media planners, we are often more concerned about how well we cover our target audience than how well we cover the total audience, which includes people who are not even prospective customers. Thus, we can apply the concept of GRP just to our target audience to figure the *target rating points* (TRP). If we have targeted correctly and selected media that go to those targets, our TRP figures should be higher than our GRP figures, which would include waste coverage; obviously, you do not want much reach or frequency to go to waste coverage.

Total Audience Impressions

Reach and frequency can also be combined into a single figure using *total audience impressions* (TAI), but using numerical reach instead of percentage reach. Let's use our same example with audience numbers instead of ratings.

Spot #	Millions of people
1	27.5
2	20.0
3	30.0
4	25.0
5	22.5
	125.0 TAI

So again we have a frequency of 5 but now with an average of 25 million audience members for each insertion. So our average numerical reach is 25 million. TAI gives us both numerical reach and frequency in a single figure.

$$25 \text{ million R} \times 5 \text{ F} = 125 \text{ million TAI}$$

So *reach* (as a number, not percentage) multiplied by *frequency* produces *total audience impressions.*

$$R\# \times F = TAI$$

Some people get confused by the fact that reach multiplied by frequency can produce both GRP and TAI. The key is to remember that using reach as a percentage produces GRP, while using reach as a number produces TAI.

The term *impression* is used to represent every time a piece of advertising is seen or heard. An audience impression is a member of the audience being exposed to your advertising one time, and here we count every time that any member of the audience is exposed to the advertising, whether it is the same person or a new audience member. These impressions are sometimes abbreviated as "imps."

Media Cost Comparisons

In addition to selecting media that reach our target, we must judge how efficient the media are, often comparing the cost of one media vehicle with another on the basis of cost efficiency. Because costs vary so much from one medium to another, these cost comparisons are usually made for one vehicle versus another, rather than one medium versus another. Only a person who is highly skilled and experienced selecting and comparing media uses these

Exhibit 2.3

An Example of Reach, Frequency, GRP, and TAI

A furniture store realizes that it cannot achieve 100 percent reach in its
local community of 50,000 population, but it would like to get close
to 100 percent. Here are the advertising results from eleven weekly
advertising insertions.

Insertion	Reach %	Reach #
1	11	5,500
2	8	4,000
3	9	4,500
4	6	3,000
5	13	6,500
6	5	2,500
7	17	8,500
8	10	5,000
9	8	4,000
10	6	3,000
11	6	3,000
F = 11	99 GRP	49,500 TAI

$$R\% \times F = GRP, \text{ so } \frac{GRP}{F} = R\%, \text{ so } \frac{99GRP}{11F} = 9\%R \text{ (avg.)}$$

$$R\# \times F = TAI, \text{ so } \frac{TAI}{F} = R\#, \text{ so } \frac{49,500\ TAI}{11\ F} = 4,500\ R \text{ (avg.}$$

$$R\% \times F = GRP, \text{ so } 9\%R \times 11F = 99GRP$$

$$R\# \times F = TAI, \text{ so } 4,500R \times 11F = 949,500TAI$$

With 99 GRP, did the store get close to its goal of 100 percent reach?
It is unlikely, unless no audience member was exposed to more than
one advertising insertion, which is doubtful. More likely, the average
audience member was exposed to perhaps three of eleven insertions,
so the percentage reach would be about 33 percent.

$$R\% \times F = GRP, \text{ so } \frac{GRP}{F} = R\%, \text{ so } \frac{99GRP}{3F} = 33\%R$$

cost comparisons to compare one medium with another. It is difficult to know whether a full-page, four-color bleed advertisement in a national magazine is equivalent to a 30-second network television commercial (called a :30), or a 60-second commercial (a :60), or perhaps a :15. It is safest, then, not to use these cost comparison figures for intermedia comparisons.

Total Impressions as One Media Standard

We have gone through how we derive total impressions from the dimensions of reach and frequency. When the media landscape was devoid of the Internet, gross impressions were a nice boxcar number that marketers used largely as sales tools. Many brand managers used these terms to sell into the grocery trade to make their media plans bigger than life. "Our media plan reaches over 36 million women," came from one sales sheet for a food brand trying to get space into a grocery chain.

Now, the Internet has made total impressions a more meaningful number, and one that is looked at with greater scrutiny. Search engine marketing is reported by total impressions. Other new media such as video games and cellular phones are sold by total impressions. Most new out-of-home media use some form of total impressions as their measuring stick for reach potential.

Total impressions are one measure that can be used regardless of the medium. As one elevates media alternatives in an ever-fragmented media landscape, total impressions are one way to compare a television campaign with an online effort with an out-of-home effort.

Online Terminology

The rapid rise in online advertising has added some new terms to the media language. While the terms are new, the principles behind them are similar to those previously discussed in the text relating to offline media.

The online term for unduplicated audiences is *unique visitors to a site*. (See Table 2.2.) For example, based on the February 2006 comScore numbers, there were a little over 17 million different online consumers who visited ESPN online. Their total impressions for the month should be higher than 17 million, since many consumers are prone to visit ESPN frequently to catch the scores of their favorite teams.

The online world has some advantages over the offline world in terms of metrics. For those measuring the offline world, you are getting audience numbers for the medium or program and not specifically for the ad you may have placed there. While there are new measures coming out that better define commercial ratings, it is certainly not a standard within the industry.

Table 2.2

An Example of Unduplicated Audiences Online

Sport Sites	Unique visitors (thousands)
ESPN	17,806
FOX Sports on MSN	15,852
Yahoo Sports	13,026
AOL Sports	11,695
NFL Internet Group	8,393

Source: 2006 Ad Age Fact Pack; comScore Media Metrics, February 2006.

Table 2.3

Prototype Online Campaign

Item	#
Total impressions	10,000,000
Click	200,000
Click rate	.02%
Applications completed	50,000
Applications conversion from click	25.0%

However, in the online world, commercial ratings exist in a manner similar to direct response advertising. An *ad click* is a measurement of a user's response to an ad that causes a redirect to another Web location or another frame or page within the ad. The *click rate* is the number of clicks divided by the total number of ad impressions. Because there are a variety of ad units now available in the online world, an ad click can be defined as a click through (taking action on the ad) or a mouse-over (placing the mouse over the ad without clicking on it.) So, as the online world evolves, it is important to get operational definitions of some of these terms, since they can have multiple meanings. Once an action has been taken on the ad, you can track this action all the way to its end result. That is called a *conversion* or *response:* people take action based on your ad to fill out an application, or go to your Web site, or purchase an item if you are offering e-commerce. (See Table 2.3.) This level of detail in terms of response is why online advertising is so popular among advertisers. It is one medium that is certainly highly measurable.

The Importance of Knowing the Universe

In this chapter we have discussed the measurement of media in terms of reach and frequency as well as total impressions. These concepts on their own are not difficult to understand, but they can become difficult to put into practical practice.

The reason why reach and frequency can be elusive is that each medium can have very different universes upon which they base their information. As one who controls the media budget, it is crucial for you to understand the basis for the numbers that are being sold to you.

For example, 99.9 percent of all households have a television set. So, if you see a 5 rating for a program, you know that 5 percent of the audience has viewed it. However, cable household penetration is hovering around 80 percent. So, a 5 rating in the cable universe is really only a 4 rating in the broader television universe, since 20 percent of the population doesn't have an opportunity to see the program.

Radio stations are likely to tout their ratings on a metro or SMSA (Standard Metropolitan Statistical Area) basis. Most metros are considerably smaller than a television DMA (Designated Marketing Area), so if you are comparing a rating between these two media, you will need to get a common ground for a meaningful comparison.

As you review online impressions, it is important to realize that as of 2005, about one-third of Americans did not have Internet access at home. However, more than 80 percent of the population has been online, gaining access through their work or at a public school or library. Again, it is important to understand the base and how the numbers are being used.

The best place to start with understanding the media universe is to understand your consumer universe and convey that universe to the media team so that everyone is on the same page. If you are a brand manager in charge of a national peanut butter brand, you are likely to have millions of users. However, if you are in charge of selling oil rig equipment, chances are that you are marketing to fewer than a thousand potential buyers. Whatever the circumstances, in today's ever-changing and expanding media world, understanding the fundamentals of your brand's customers and their media habits will pay dividends.

Chapter 3

Learning About Media Costs

Understanding Media Costs

Once you understand the audience of a medium or a media vehicle, the reckoning of media planning comes on assessing its value. Media planning and negotiating are based on judging how efficient media are and comparing the cost of one media vehicle with another.

In the advertising industry, there are *absolute costs* and *relative costs*. Absolute costs, sometimes called unit costs or vehicle costs, refer to what you are going to pay for the media placement. A full-page advertisement in the national edition of the *Wall Street Journal* costs approximately $180,000. Running a 30-second commercial during the Super Bowl costs approximately $2 million. Buying a local radio commercial in Sherman, Texas, might cost $40. So, unit costs vary widely and are based largely on the total number of impressions that the individual media vehicle delivers and the value that advertisers place on those impressions.

That brings us to relative costs. It is important to understand the relative efficiency of the Super Bowl and the *Wall Street Journal*. Without such an understanding, how would you know what the best value is? To compare one media vehicle to another and one medium to another, the gold standard in media cost comparison is *cost per thousand* or CPM.

Cost per Thousand (CPM)

In advertising, the number 1,000 can be abbreviated as K (*kilo*) or M (*mille*). Most often, K is used for money and M is used for audiences. Because 1,000 × 1,000 equals a million, we use MM to mean a million. (Do not be confused by media headlines, which often abbreviate million using just one M.)

All this is a bit of background to explain the abbreviation of "cost per thousand" as CPM. With that little history lesson under our belt, we can put the CPM term to work. CPM is a mainstay for comparing one media vehicle to another, as well as comparing one medium to another. Let's start off by looking at how to use CPM to compare one media vehicle to another.

It can be difficult to compare one media vehicle to another because you must take into account the advertising unit rates or prices along with the reach or impressions that they deliver. Let's say that you are looking at two different magazines that have different unit rates and different circulations. Say that Magazine A, with a circulation of 2.1 million, charges $23,500 for a full-page advertisement, and that Magazine B, with a circulation of 1.2 million, charges $13,500 for the same full-page ad. You might expect that the magazine with the larger circulation charges more since costs rise as you reach more people, but is it the more economical way to reach your audience?

This is where CPM comes into play. Instead of trying to compare the cost and circulations at the same time, we assume that each magazine has a circulation of only 1,000. We compare the cost for each 1,000 circulation by dividing the advertising rate by the circulation to get the cost of advertising in a single copy of the publication. Then we multiply the answer by 1,000 to compare the cost of a thousand-copy circulation.

Here is the CPM for Magazine A:

$$\text{Magazine A} = \frac{\$23,500}{2,100,000} \times 1,000 = \$11.19 \text{ CPM}$$

Doing the same for the other publication gives a comparison CPM.

$$\text{Magazine B} = \frac{\$13,500}{1,200,000} \times 1,000 = \$11.25 \text{ CPM}$$

So, based on this CPM analysis, Magazine A has a CPM based on its circulation of $11.19 while Magazine B has a CPM of $11.25. In this case, the CPMs are virtually identical. Since Magazine A has a 75 percent higher circulation than Magazine B and is priced at relatively the same cost as the smaller circulation publication, Magazine A seems to be the better value of the two.

CPM is used in every media analysis from print to broadcast to on-line. The only difference between the various media is the method used to calculate the audience. Raw circulation figures are typically used as a point of comparison for print, while audience estimates are used for broadcast and online audience figures. However, the same analysis can

Table 3.1

Media CPM Based on Adults

Medium	CPM
TV	$25.00
Magazine	$12.50
Radio	$9.50
Newspaper	$35.00
Outdoor	$5.00
Online	$20.00

Source: 2006 FKM.

be performed whether you are comparing two Web sites or two television programs.

CPM as an Intermedia Comparison Analysis

It is difficult even for the most seasoned media professional to compare one medium to another. Is a full-page, four-color bleed advertisement in a magazine the equivalent of a 30-second network television commercial? Or is the placement in a video game worth the same as a banner ad on a gaming enthusiasts' Web site? These are difficult questions, and while there is some research in the area of intermedia comparisons, much of it remains proprietary.

In the case of intermedia comparisons, CPM is a standard to review but certainly should not be the last analysis. The following is a general CPM estimate for a wide variety of media.

As you can see, if you were selecting based on CPM alone, outdoor would be the medium of choice. However, of the media listed in Table 3.1, outdoor has the lowest advertising revenue. So, while it has a low CPM, advertisers are voting with their dollars on other media.

As a brand manager looking at the media landscape, you will work with your media group to determine the impact of each medium for your particular brand. The impact value of each medium can then be compared to the CPM or used to weigh the CPM for a more definitive analysis.

For example, if you feel that an outdoor ad has the same impact as a television commercial, then you can purchase considerably more outdoor impressions for the dollar than television. However, if you feel that television is worth 10 times the value of outdoor ads, then outdoor may not be such a good bargain.

The following is an example of weighing CPMs based on an impact score for

Table 3.2

Delight Salad Dressing
CPM Adjusted by Media Impact Weights

Medium	CPM	Media Impact	Adjusted CPM
TV	$20.00	100	$20.00
Magazine	$10.00	70	$14.30
Radio	$8.00	30	$24.00
Newspaper	$30.00	50	$60.00
Outdoor	$5.00	10	$50.00
Online	$20.00	40	$50.00

Note: Media Impact score 1 to 100.

each medium for a package goods brand. (See Table 3.2.) The goal of the brand is to convey appetite appeal and to demonstrate how it is used in a wide variety of situations.

The CPM is the standard measure for comparing media, but it should not be used within a vacuum. It provides the basis for determining value but is not the only aspect to assigning value to a medium.

Cost per Point

CPM is the main cost comparison criteria when looking at a variety of media, but planners working with broadcast costs on a national and local basis use a standard called *cost per point* (CPP). A cost per point compares broadcast vehicles on the basis of how much it costs to reach 1 percent of the audience. Remember that 1 percent reach is the same as a rating point, so we call this comparison cost per point.

Let's take a look at how you might use a CPP in comparing two radio stations. If radio station A costs $5,300 per commercial unit and reaches 2.2 percent of our audience (the rating), we simply divide the cost by the rating to derive the CPP.

$$CPP = \frac{\$5,300}{2.2 \text{ Rtg}} = \$2,409 \text{ CPP}$$

If you looked at radio station B, which charges $6,200 per unit and achieves a rating of 2.5 percent, its CPP would be as follows:

$$CPP = \frac{\$6,200}{2.5 \text{ Rtg}} = \$2,480 \text{ CPP}$$

Table 3.3

Daytime TV Local Costs for Bob's Baked Beans

Market	DMA Rank	Women 18–49 Daytime CPP
New York City	1	$798
Dallas/Fort Worth	7	$303
Buffalo, NY	44	$65
Boise, ID	157	$40
Victoria, BC	204	$20
Total		$1,223

Source: Spot Quotations and Data (SQAD).

So, in this example, radio station A is slightly more efficient in reaching a rating point (1 percent of the audience) than radio station B. When media negotiators are rapidly calculating hundreds of programs and stations, the CPP is a key measure for efficiency. Think of it as the currency for local broadcast negotiations.

The reason that CPP is used in broadcast planning instead of CPM is that it is a much simpler method of assessing costs across various markets or across various dayparts. CPM is a great analysis tool to determine value, as is CPP; however, CPP allows for the quick addition of costs across various markets. If you were planning to advertise in the top five media markets in the United States in daytime television, you would not want to add up all the hundreds of possibilities of unit costs for this television period across all these markets. The CPP allows you to quickly figure costs by taking into account the size of the market, since 1 percent of the population of New York is a lot bigger than 1 percent of the population of Boise. The following is an example of how media planners use CPP to add up media costs for a local market campaign. (See Table 3.3.)

Online Cost Analysis

As we stated previously, the online media world offers some much deeper diagnostics than most other media. However, the CPM is the initial standard for all online analysis whether it is in search engine marketing or in traditional online advertising.

The second layer of cost analysis beyond the CPM is the *cost per click* (CPC). The cost per click is calculated by simply dividing the media cost by the number of clicks obtained within a certain time frame. Most online media professionals analyze their online plans after a week or two of activity to determine what sites and what creative executions are producing the lowest CPC. Then adjustments are made to the subsequent schedules to (1) add more impressions to proven performers, (2) eliminate costly performing sites, or (3) add contingency sites to the campaign.

Depending upon the category, online media planners will negotiate with the Web sites on a CPC basis or on a *cost per lead* basis (CPL). For example, if the advertisers know that they will make money if their campaign hits a certain cost per lead target (say $20), then they will negotiate with the Web publishers to pay for that target response and to not pay for leads above that threshold. For established categories with known conversion rates such as auto insurance, this is a standard method for online placement. It ties in nicely with search engine marketing pricing, which is done on a bid basis for selective keywords. The more popular the keyword, the more it may cost. For example, the insurance business is highly competitive online, so a keyword such as "auto insurance" could command as much as $200 per click. On the other hand, a lower interest category, such as hazardous waste hauling, may be only $10 per click.

Some online media planners also use the term *cost per action* (CPA) to describe the cost of generating a sale, acquiring a customer, or making some sort of transaction. Again, this is calculated by dividing the online campaign cost by the action that it is designed to generate.

Cost Trade-offs

Going back to the beginning of this chapter, we discussed the two kinds of cost analysis: the initial analysis is absolute costs and the second is relative costs. These two pillars of media value analysis are used by media planners in their ongoing evaluation of determining the best media plan for the dollar.

As a brand manager in charge of media dollars, it is important to ask a variety of questions regarding media costs. The first question is: What can I do effectively for the dollars that I have to invest in media? This is not asking what the best CPM is, but what the best media plan is. Let's take a look at an example for a national package goods brand on a $1 million budget. Here are three plans developed for the same product by different media agencies:

1. Plan A was developed by a CPM-driven agency, which said that the brand should schedule national television spots for eight weeks within the daytime television daypart, with approximately 40 TRPs per week or 15 to 20 commercials per week.
2. Plan B recommended only magazines as the support plan. Their

plan consisted of six months of support using six publications with four insertions per publication or a total of 24 insertions.

3. Plan C recommended allocating the dollars to the six best markets for the brand to develop a television and print support plan that would cover 75 percent of the year with activity.

Based on the question of effectiveness, which of these plans do you feel meets the criteria? Do you get the same answer if you ask the question, Which plan is the most cost efficient?

Common sense would tell you that while Plan A might be cost efficient, it may not be very effective. On the other hand, Plan C may be the most effective but it might be too limiting in terms of sales and efficiency. And so, there you have the trade-offs that happen with every media plan and negotiation. There is always a trade-off between what can be done well and what is most efficient for the brand.

As you assess media plans, it is important to understand the fundamentals of cost analysis, but it is even more important to understand the fundamentals of trade-off analysis.

Chapter 4
The Media and Their Characteristics

There are plenty of factors other than costs on which to compare advertising media. In fact, if you rely solely on advertising rates and costs, you are likely to place your advertising in front of an unresponsive audience. Let's look at some of the most commonly used characteristics as they are used in advertising media analysis and selection.

Audience Qualities

What is the audience like? Are the audience members similar to one another (homogeneous), or are they very different from one another (heterogeneous)? It makes sense that it is easier to reach a homogeneous audience than a heterogeneous one; people who are alike tend to do the same kinds of activities and pay attention to the same kinds of media offerings.

Demographics

Are the audience members rich or poor, employed or idle, well-educated or dropouts? Of course, these descriptions are the extremes, but these demographic characteristics are important. Demography is the study of populations, so demographic characteristics are population factors: age, income, gender, educational level, employment, number of children at home, whether urban or rural, and the like.

It is easier to sell a Lexus 400 to someone with a sizable income than to someone who barely scrapes by each month. The Great Books series is likely to be purchased by someone who has a college education. Sweetened breakfast cereal is sold mostly to households with young children.

Of course, there are other ways to segment a media audience in addition to demographics. These methods include psychographics, based on psychological differences, and sociographics, based on social and cultural differences.

Audiences can also be segmented according to heavy and light users of a product or service, or by lifestyle, which will be discussed later. Other segmentation patterns include such geographic segments as parts of the country or urban versus rural, and a combination of such elements as geodemographics, a combination of geography and demography; for example, the U.S. Navy may find good enlistment prospects in such landlocked states as Montana and North Dakota because of a combination of population factors and geographic factors.

Activities and Habits

Certain media types and vehicles reach certain audiences. Magazines are read mostly by those with good incomes and educations, while television is viewed by almost everyone, although the lower-income groups spend more of their time with broadcast media. Even within a media type, there are differences: all kinds of men watch football games on television, but televised golf matches are viewed mostly by men with good jobs and high incomes.

Audience Involvement

Do members of the audience pay close attention to a particular medium, or are they somewhat remote and removed from media involvement? People may have the radio playing as background, not giving it their full attention, but sit down in the evening to watch television with no outside distractions. Some people scan a newspaper while others read it carefully. A person driving down a highway may not give much notice to a billboard, but another person caught in a traffic tie-up on the same road has several minutes to read and remember the billboard message.

Along with involvement, a related factor involves distractions. We know that people who view prime-time television in the evening hours pay closer attention than do people who watch daytime television. One reason for this difference is that there are more distractions during the daytime: telephone calls, children's needs, meal planning, and the like. Another reason may be the increased number of commercial messages during daytime television, which provides more opportunities to leave the television set in order to complete chores.

Influentials vs. Followers

Within your circle of family and friends is there someone who always seems to know about the latest movies, someone else who is knowledgeable about politics, and yet another person who keeps up with current clothing style trends or music or current events? If these knowledgeable individuals tell others about their opinions, they may be "influentials," while those who listen to and heed their advice may be "followers."

Many advertisers try to select advertising media that reach influentials, in hopes of persuading these individuals to learn about products and services and then tell others about them. Other advertisers want to use media that reach followers, using the media to play the role of influential to persuade these followers to listen to and obey the advertising message; still other advertisers may avoid using these same media, believing that followers are persuaded more by influentials than by the media.

Lifestyle

Different people have different lifestyles. Some want to acquire physical goods while others want to live in rustic settings with few possessions. Some people read many magazines and watch little television, while others do just the opposite.

Lifestyle impacts people's tendency to purchase certain kinds of products. It is useless to try to sell beer to teetotalers, but it is fairly easy to sell electronic gear to those who want the latest computers, sound systems, and telephones. Some media vehicles appeal to one kind of lifestyle while others attract a completely different lifestyle.

Media Attributes

Advertisers use many factors other than the audience in their media analyses and plans. Several of these attributes are characteristics of the mass media themselves.

Cost

Obviously, media costs are a major consideration. Some media are expensive while others are less so; television has high advertising rates for air time, and the cost of producing a television commercial may also be steep. Radio, on the other hand, is much less expensive. Although costs are important, the costs must be balanced against all the other factors. Does an inexpensive medium have the same audience impact, or is there a trade-off for the less expensive media outlet?

Most advertising media also offer discounts, which can be based on the amount of advertising purchased—a "quantity discount"—or on regular purchases of advertising—a "frequency discount."

Exhibit 4.1

Intermedia Comparisons

Several references have been made to intermedia comparisons, such as comparing radio with television, or television with magazines.

It should be obvious that a thirty-second (called a :30 in the business) radio commercial does not carry the same impact as a :30 on television. The television medium combines sight and sound and offers motion and, thus, demonstration. Not only does television provide more impact than does radio, but these added dimensions of television also offer more creative breadth.

At some point, however, more radio may be equivalent to television; maybe two or five or eight commercials on radio carry a weight equal to one commercial on television. And radio advertising tends to cost much less than television advertising does, so it might be used to attain more reach and frequency in exchange for the lessened impact.

Similarly, does a :30 on network television equal a full-page advertisement in a national magazine, or a full-page with color, or a full-page with both color and bleed—or what? The problem is that every individual brand's case is unique, and it is difficult to project an answer from past history. Although selective companies may have proprietary research regarding the value of one medium versus another, there is a dearth of published research on the topic. As you see in Table 4.1, most of the published research was in the 1960s and early 1970s. Its historical relevance to today's issues is questionable, plus there is no consensus in the research itself.

For all these reasons, it is unwise for novice marketers and media planners to involve themselves with intermedia comparisons. It is far safer to compare one media vehicle with another, say, one radio station with another, or one television network with the others, or one group of magazines with several others. However, more and more companies are using sophisticated marketing-mix analyses to help them judge the value and economic benefits of their advertising media plans.

Cost Efficiency

As we saw in the previous chapter, there are various measures of cost efficiency, such as cost per thousand (CPM) and cost per rating point (CPP).

Table 4.1

Summary of Classic Television vs. Print or Radio Advertising Impact Studies

Sponsor/Date	Methodology	Findings
CBS TV Network/1960–61	Teen spies observe TV and magazine ad exposure among adults, ask brand awareness/desire to buy questions before and after exposure	TV ad exposures in prime time generate double the brand awareness gains than magazine ads and 3-4 times the desire to buy
Look/1962–63	Telephone recall studies of *Look* subscribers and prime-time TV viewers	Page 4C ads outscored TV :60s, 24 percent to 18 percent in verified recall for six advertisers
Life/1968–69	Telephone recall studies of *Life* subscribers and prime-time TV viewers	Page 4C ads outscored TV :30s and :60s by 45 percent to 50 percent for seven advertisers
C.E. Hooper, Inc./1968–69	Telephone coincidental studies of persons just exposed to TV, radio, magazines, newspapers; ability to name last brand ad seen/heard	TV outscored radio 19 percent to 14 percent but trailed behind magazines (34 percent) and newspapers (23 percent)
Gallup-Robinson/1960s–70s	Invited viewing and reading copy tests using 24-hour recall	TV scores twice as high as magazines in verified recall
AAAA/1964	Adults claiming ad exposure to TV, radio, magazines, and newspapers rated them on several criteria	TV commercials were rated as predominantly enjoyable (38 percent) and informative (21 percent), but 31 percent found them annoying or offensive. In contrast, only 15 percent of magazines and 18 percent of newspaper ads were rated negatively.
ABC/CBS/NBC/1970–71	Adults exposed to TV commercials and magazine ads. Criterion: Pre-/post-coupon redemption claims (vs. "control") for twelve brands.	TV commercials induced 82 percent greater increments in advertised brand coupon redemption than magazine ads

Source: 2007 FKM agency research.

Efficiency in media is usually a solid advertising media goal, and many advertisers try to consider cost efficiencies as well as the basic costs of advertising. Keep in mind that many cost efficiency ratios are used only for comparing one vehicle with another but within the same general media type, and that intermedia comparisons of cost efficiencies require careful limits and provisos as well as much experience and caution. (See Exhibit 4.1.)

Reach

One major factor is reach. How many of the target group are communicated to by a certain medium or vehicle (numerical reach), or what part of the target group sees or hears that medium or vehicle (percentage reach)?

A media vehicle that reaches more of the target audience is usually desirable, but that vehicle may also cost more. So many factors must be considered together: reach, cost, cost efficiency, and other factors.

Frequency

Because frequency is often an essential advertising media goal, media that offer frequency at reasonable rates are usually under consideration. Some media offer frequency as an almost natural part of their package; broadcast media are known for advertisements that appear frequently, and the Internet is available every minute of every day. Newspapers appear less frequently, and magazines even less so. Keep in mind, however, that there are two kinds of frequency: frequency of insertion and frequency of exposure. No audience member will be exposed to your advertisement every time it runs.

If you need more information about reach, frequency, cost efficiency, and similar basic media terms, look back at chapter 2.

Irritation Factor

Along with high frequency comes the risk of irritating the audience. People who see or hear an advertisement too often may turn it off in their minds or, even worse, develop a negative reaction to that message. Irritation most often occurs with disruptive and annoying advertisements, but it can happen with any advertising message. The Internet, television, and radio cause the most advertising irritation because messages may be disruptive, are presented often, and are beyond the audience member's control. If an advertisement were to appear on several pages of a newspaper, the reader would only have to turn the pages to avoid it, and turning pages is a regular part of newspaper reading. But if an advertisement appears several times an evening on a cable

network, the viewer would have to switch stations or stop viewing to avoid
the commercial.

Color

For some advertisements, color is crucial. Portraying fashion items may need
color, and showing a detergent box may require special colors. Color quality
is generally good in most magazines, but not so good in many newspapers.
Television and Internet color can be good, but color quality also relies on
the type of reception and appliance used by the audience members.

Motion and Demonstration

To demonstrate a product or service, motion may be necessary. Media such
as television, motion pictures, and the Internet may therefore be required.
The choices are limited, because few media can demonstrate or provide
motion well.

Scheduling

When your advertisements appear is an important factor, and some media
permit more scheduling flexibility than do others. There are several components of scheduling:

Exposure

Running a television advertisement during prime time will bring more audience exposure than will a daytime commercial, because more people watch
television at night, and they have fewer distractions then. A print insertion
in a building design magazine may reach many architects in February, when
they are planning for the coming building season by consulting sources for
the newest and best materials, but it will reach fewer architects in August,
when they are likely to be out examining the actual construction sites and
have little time to read.

Flexibility

An Internet advertisement appears at any time that an audience member calls
up that Web site. A television or radio station can schedule advertising at
any hour of the day. Newspapers cannot offer advertising at any particular
hour, but daily newspapers can offer any day. Magazines may offer only

weekly or monthly schedules, which provide for less flexibility in scheduling the advertising.

Waves

Scheduling in waves can help avoid the irritation factor and can keep an advertising campaign fresher for a longer time. It can also save money by extending the campaign over a longer period.

The high point in the waves is the period of intense advertising, called a "flight saturation" or simply a "flight." A period of low advertising intensity or of no advertising is known as a "hiatus." If there is a level of moderate advertising after a period of waves, it is called a "sustaining period."

Preparation Time

How much time do you have to perfect your campaign before it appears in the media? Magazines often require that advertising placements reach them weeks or even months in advance of publication. On the other hand, it may be possible to call a radio station and have an announcement read on the air within an hour or so, if time is still available for purchase.

Availabilities and Preemptions

In broadcast media, there is only so much time to sell. If another advertiser has already reserved a particular time, it is no longer available; you must choose from the remaining available time slots, which are known as "availabilities" or "avails."

Some broadcast stations offer preemptible time at a discounted rate. If another advertiser comes along and offers the full price, your advertising will be preempted: either it will not run or it will be shifted to another time slot.

Availabilities are not pertinent to print media because there is little limit to the number of advertisements; if more advertisements are purchased, more pages will be printed, resulting in a larger issue. In fact, the number of advertisements in a newspaper or magazine is usually the determining factor in how many pages that issue will comprise.

Coverage

Previously we covered audience factors. Coverage is basically the same kind of consideration but from a media perspective rather than an audience viewpoint. Certain media do a better job of covering certain audiences.

For example, daytime television dramas and talk shows do a good job of covering female heads of households, but a relatively poor job of reaching male teens who are employed full-time. On the other hand, rock music radio formats reach male teens but not older, retired persons.

Selectivity

Selectivity is related to coverage. If you desire coverage of a certain demographic group, you may have a wide choice of media options, but some of those will also cover many kinds of people other than your primary target. Selectivity offers coverage without as much waste; you select media that cover your target group well but without a lot of coverage to groups in whom you are not interested.

Responsiveness

Some consumers respond to some media types better than they do to others. For example, a coupon may elicit a much greater response from a mother with a large family, who must stretch the family purchasing dollars, than one with a smaller family. In fact, every medium has groups of consumers who respond better to it than others. Many packaged-goods marketers are now using a part of their marketing-mix analysis to determine the responsiveness for each medium by different target groups.

Relevance

In today's increasingly fragmented media world, media exist that are certainly on target for specific audiences and products. For example, the Food Network is a cable network devoted to the making of great meals. If you have a product that is marketed to people who like to cook, this is a likely match. The same can be said for magazines such as *Good Housekeeping* or *Gourmet,* where recipe ideas are a major part of the editorial content. In fact, the media vehicle can actually become a marketplace unto itself. *Vogue* magazine devotes as much as 75 percent of an issue to advertising, yet consumers are looking at these advertisements to make their fashion decisions.

Support for Other Media

Certain advertising media are of questionable efficacy when used on their own, but work well in combination with other media.

For example, if demonstration is required, radio might not be an appropriate choice, but radio might well be used to combine with and supplement the demonstrations shown in television commercials. If the same themes, messages, music, and words are used in both media, the radio commercials will extend the impact of the television ads, gaining both reach and frequency at a lesser expense. Similarly, transit and outdoor advertising are generally noticed only in passing, which may not be enough for a complicated message, but which might be quite good to remind audience members of the messages carried through other media.

Audience Portrayal Through Media

Another media characteristic combines media and audience factors: how the audience is portrayed through the media. Many television commercials, for example, portray users of the product or service being promoted, and from these portrayals the audience members learn what kinds of people are being targeted and what uses and benefits they might gain from purchase of the service or product. If people see themselves in a commercial, they may feel that they should also use the advertised item. Earlier, we discussed audience involvement, which might also be a combination of audience and media factors.

Slice-of-life commercials, which act as though the scene being shown is part of people's everyday lives, actually are based on portrayals of persons using the advertised product or service. In contrast, a hard sell utilizes strong messages aimed at convincing the audience to consider buying; these strong arguments are likely to be delivered by an announcer or spokesperson, which diminishes the opportunity to portray real users. Both types of portrayals are also used in other media, but television provides a handy and universal example.

Of course, other factors are also likely to come into play in planning and selecting the media for an advertising campaign. Among the most obvious are the marketing objectives themselves, which will be discussed in the next chapter. Then, in subsequent chapters, we'll consider other factors in detail, such as the audience, geography, and timing.

Exhibit 4.2

Newspaper Advertising

Advantages
- ❖ Timely
- ❖ Contents vital to audience; thus, good readership
- ❖ Broad reach; appeal to all kinds of people
- ❖ Localized circulation; can target geographically
- ❖ Complete coverage; almost everyone reads newspapers
- ❖ Edited for all ages; can reach adults, teens, men, women
- ❖ Frequent publication; daily advertising results in continuous impressions
- ❖ Can handle emergency situations; short ordering time
- ❖ Can tie in advertisements with news
- ❖ Can direct customers to stores
- ❖ All sizes of advertising budgets can use newspapers
- ❖ Quick results
- ❖ Can include many different items in a single advertisement
- ❖ Reader controls exposure (as opposed to radio or television)

Disadvantages
- ❖ Many differences in sizes, deadlines, etc., so advertiser must have separate dealings with each newspaper; can be costly to change mechanical specifications for each newspaper (however, can utilize standard advertising units)
- ❖ Great variation in production quality
- ❖ Color may be of poor quality or difficult to use
- ❖ Short life
- ❖ Hasty reading

Exhibit 4.3

Consumer Magazine Advertising

Advantages
- ❖ Reader lingers over editorial and advertising matter; gives longer time to sell
- ❖ High quality of production and color; can show package
- ❖ Flexible scheduling: weeklies, monthlies, etc.
- ❖ Selective readership; permits market segmentation
- ❖ Prestige of the medium, in many cases
- ❖ Advertising message retained for a long time; has long life
- ❖ Better audience data than from most other media
- ❖ Flexibility in format: size, foldout, insert, color, smell, etc.

Disadvantages
- ❖ Waste circulation, especially in general consumer magazines
- ❖ Advertisements easily ignored, compared to television or radio

Exhibit 4.4

Business Publication Advertising

Advantages
- ❖ Appeal to business interests; no frills, thus avid readership
- ❖ Often read during business hours; reader's mind on business
- ❖ No distractions; no other news or entertainment material
- ❖ Produce direct inquiries, from people who have that concern and responsibility
- ❖ Flexibility in timing and format, same as consumer magazines

Disadvantages
- ❖ Lots of other competitive advertising

Exhibit 4.5

Television Advertising

Advantages
- ❖ Demonstration
- ❖ Impact; combination of sight and sound
- ❖ Mass coverage
- ❖ Extensive viewer time; people spend a lot of time in front of the television set
- ❖ Repetition; better and easier than for print
- ❖ Flexibility: of coverage, of commercial content
- ❖ Prestige of the medium
- ❖ Versatile: sound effects, color, motion, stills, voices, etc.
- ❖ Hard to tune out a commercial message; broadcaster controls exposure, to some degree
- ❖ Personal involvement of audience members
- ❖ Techniques of television advertising are so effective they are used for educational purposes, e.g., *Sesame Street*

Disadvantages
- ❖ Control in the hands of telecaster and audience, not the advertiser
- ❖ Cost can be very high
- ❖ Mortality rate; commercials get old quickly
- ❖ Distrust of "personal selling"; print advertisements carry more of a stamp of authenticity
- ❖ Lack of selectivity; the mass audience can be a disadvantage as well as an advantage

Exhibit 4.6

Radio Advertising

Advantages
- ❖ Timely, flexible
- ❖ Can be economical
- ❖ Penetration into all homes and all rooms; dorms, kitchens, etc.
- ❖ Complements other media; can reiterate and supplement campaign
- ❖ Useful for reaching specialized audiences: farm, foreign-language, ethnic, etc.
- ❖ Strong on-air personality can build large audience of listeners
- ❖ Daily continuity, which may be too expensive in other media
- ❖ Penetration into suburbs
- ❖ Can make excellent use of slogans, music, sound effects
- ❖ At the moment of impact, there is no competition; especially good for small retailers
- ❖ Can reach people anywhere: in cars, on picnics, at the beach, while exercising
- ❖ Good for merchandising; can tie in with promotions

Disadvantages
- ❖ Perishable
- ❖ Rate policies not standardized; must deal with each individual station
- ❖ Advertisements can be easily ignored

Exhibit 4.7

Direct Mail Advertising/Direct Marketing

Advantages
- ❖ Selectivity
- ❖ Intense coverage is possible
- ❖ Speed and timing are controllable
- ❖ Flexibility of format: color, premiums, gifts, smells, etc.
- ❖ Can involve the customer: pencil, prize, multiple sheets, cut-outs, stamps
- ❖ Can include complete information, even a sample
- ❖ Can be personalized
- ❖ No waste circulation is necessary

Disadvantages
- ❖ High cost per thousand and cost per point
- ❖ Difficult to maintain a current and effective mailing list
- ❖ Customer resistance; neither editorial content nor entertainment to attract and pacify audience

Exhibit 4.8

Outdoor Advertising

Advantages
- ❖ Reaches potential customers close to point of sale
- ❖ Communication can be quick and simple
- ❖ Repetition easy in high-traffic areas

Disadvantages
- ❖ Short message may limit creative breadth
- ❖ Despoiling the landscape; may earn public's enmity
- ❖ Legal restrictions

Exhibit 4.9

Transit Advertising

Advantages
- ❖ Economical; very low cost per thousand
- ❖ High repetition
- ❖ Continuous exposure, day and night
- ❖ Limited number of competitive messages
- ❖ Captive audience

Disadvantages
- ❖ People are not thinking of advertising; hurrying elsewhere
- ❖ Advertisements subject to mutilation and vandalism
- ❖ Some doubts as to quality of the market

Exhibit 4.10

Point-of-Purchase Advertising

Advantages
- ❖ Take advantage of preselling in other media
- ❖ May help secure better locations in store; may require "spiff" or "push" money
- ❖ Reaches people who are ready to buy
- ❖ Can trigger impulse buying

Disadvantages
- ❖ May be difficult to gain store cooperation
- ❖ Hard to control quality or location of display areas

Exhibit 4.11

Internet Advertising

Advantages
- ❖ One-to-one communication
- ❖ Heavy users receive heavy exposure
- ❖ Flexibility
- ❖ High-income audience
- ❖ Interactivity; personal involvement of audience
- ❖ Selectivity

Also see advantages under Exhibit 4.5, Television Advertising, and Exhibit 4.7, Direct Mail/Direct Marketing.

Disadvantages
- ❖ Cost is high: high CPM and CPP
- ❖ Easy to ignore, especially banner advertisements

Also see disadvantages under Exhibit 4.5, Television Advertising, and Exhibit 4.7, Direct Mail/Direct Marketing.

Chapter 5

How Marketing Objectives Impact Media Planning

Never, under any conditions, should you begin an advertising media plan without first establishing your objectives. But establishing objectives for your media effort is not the first thing you should do.

This seemingly contradictory advice is not really so puzzling after all. You should establish your objectives before you begin any planning effort, whether in media or in any other aspect of your marketing program. Yet the media objectives rely on other objectives, and those other objectives must be established prior to laying out your media objectives.

Objectives: Marketing, Advertising, Then Media

Always begin by establishing the overall marketing objectives. Then set separate advertising objectives, which must be in concert with and derived from the overall marketing objectives. Finally, set the media objectives, which are based on the advertising objectives, which, as we just saw, are based on the marketing objectives. Again, the advertising media objectives will be stated separately from the other objectives, but they will derive from and will support both the advertising objectives and the marketing objectives. Advertising media do not operate in a vacuum; they must be part of the overall marketing and advertising plans.

Along with media objectives, you are likely to include specific advertising message objectives and perhaps research, production or other types of objectives for your advertising campaign.

Based on Research

Ideally, all objectives will be based on research. Be wary if someone proposes to use advertising media, or to use advertising at all, without first doing research. Some people seem to have an innate feeling or sixth sense about advertising and media, but they are not really operating without research foundations; instead, they are using their own experience and expertise, which are a type of research, based on the results of past efforts. And that, after all, is a basic kind of research.

Most people, however, must make manifest research efforts. You draw up a list of questions to which you need the answers, and then you design or contract for research that will provide insights into those answers.

Perhaps surprisingly, the research questions may not include such questions as "What advertising media should we use in the upcoming campaign?" Instead, questions may focus on the best kinds of people to target or the best kinds of locations in which to market. The answers to these questions will help you derive your target markets and target groups and, then, your media selections.

Utilizing research makes the task much easier when it is time to establish the marketing, advertising, and media objectives.

Objectives as a Road Map

Imagine that you are in Kansas City and you want to drive to Tulsa. Unless you are familiar with the route, you would likely consult a road map.

When you look at the map, you first find Kansas City, then you find Tulsa, and on the map you might work your way back from Tulsa to Kansas City. If you just start out driving from Kansas City, you have no idea which way to go: north, south, east, west, or, in this case, southwest. So knowing where you already are is important, but knowing that alone is not enough. You need to know your destination, too.

If you track back from Tulsa to Kansas City, you are working from your objective back to your starting point. That is not the way you will drive it; you will drive just the reverse, from Kansas City to Tulsa. But you will plot your course from the destination back to the point of origin.

That's the way you make a plan work, too, whether it is a marketing plan, an advertising plan, or a media plan. You know your point of origin, and then you set up your objectives. Finally, you plan how to make your way from the origination point to the objective, and you often do it by working backward to find out what is needed to meet your goals.

Objectives, Strategies, and Tactics

So far, we have used the term "objectives" for the place where you wish to go. Sometimes the term "goals" will be used. In advertising, objectives are

Exhibit 5.1

Contingency Plans

Perhaps the best time to prepare for next year's taxes is right after you finish this year's taxes. That way, you'll have all your documents and figures, and you will know what you wish you had done better for the current year.

Similarly, the best time to do a contingency media plan is right after the proposed media plan has been completed. That way, you have all your documents and figures, and you are well aware of the other options that came to mind.

A contingency plan is not the same as a reserve fund. A reserve takes part of the advertising media budget and sets it aside for unanticipated emergencies. Doing that indicates two negative ideas: you are not confident about your proposed plan, and you don't need your entire budget.

A better strategy is a contingency plan, which is an alternative to the plan that has been proposed. Rather than setting aside budgeted monies, it allows for transfers among media choices.

Contingency plans usually answer three questions, all of which start with the same phrase: What will you do during the year if . . . ? The questions are these:

1. What will you do during the year if sales expectations are not being met?
2. What will you do during the year if sales expectations are being exceeded?
3. What will you do during the year if a competitor takes some unexpected action?

If the campaign proposal is for some period other than a year, substitute "during the campaign period" for "during the year."

The more complete and accurate you can make your contingency plans, the better. If they are actually needed, it will likely be an emergency situation, so you will not have time to re-do media plans or to finalize details. You need contingency plans that you can put into action on short notice.

what you want to accomplish in the long term and goals are what you want to accomplish in the short term. In business, the short term is usually within the coming year, and the long term applies to things beyond the coming year. Use this vocabulary consistently with your coworkers.

Most of the time, you will have a five-year plan, which is the long term, with details for the coming year, which is the short term. Each year, you will update the short-term goals and plans, and then extend the long-term plans and objectives for another year, always working about five years ahead. Whether it is three years or five years or ten years does not matter so much as the fact that you always have short-term and long-term achievements and plans, and that they are updated regularly—because things often change rapidly in advertising, the long-range plans may be for a shorter period and the updating may occur more often.

So objectives and goals are what you want to achieve. The plans that you establish to meet these objectives and goals are called strategies. Then, the implementation or execution of those plans is the tactics. Remember that distinction. Tactics are putting the plans into action.

You always have these three stages: first, objectives and goals, what you want to achieve; second, your strategies, the plans to achieve those goals and objectives; and third, the tactics, by which you implement your plans.

Advertising Media Are Strategies, Not Objectives

Even though you will eventually establish media objectives and goals, the advertising media themselves are not objectives or goals. Media are strategies.

Your advertising media goals may be to reach a certain number of persons, with a certain frequency, with some impact. The media goal is not to use newspapers or television or outdoor billboards. The media themselves are strategies; they are ways that you plan to achieve those goals of reach, frequency, and impact, and maybe continuity, cost efficiency, and creative considerations.

Keep this distinction in mind. Media are strategies, not goals or objectives. Do not establish goals to use certain media. Instead, establish goals of things that you hope to accomplish with your advertising media, and leave the actual media selection to the strategy stage.

Why make this differentiation? Because if you establish the use of certain types of media as part of your goals, you are setting out on your trip without knowing where you want to go. It would be like driving in any direction from Kansas City, on any highway, without knowing in which direction is Tulsa. If you spell out the media as goals, you are likely to overlook some good alternatives, because your mind is already made up.

Make this a three-stage process. First, set your media goals and objectives, without detailing which actual media might be used. Then plan how to achieve the goals and objectives, using the best types of media. Finally, implement the plan and execute the actual advertising campaign.

Setting Good Objectives

Good goals and objectives, then, help you determine where you want to go with your marketing, advertising, and media efforts. So setting good objectives and goals is crucial to success.

Good objectives usually use the infinitive form of a verb, as in "to do" something. Your objectives might be to accomplish, to sell, to convince, to change, to increase, to communicate, to eliminate, to compete, to modify, to promote, to reach, or to do any of a host of other things, or some combination of these things.

Note that the advertising media themselves could not possibly be objectives and goals because they are not verbs. You could not have "to newspaper" or "to outdoor" as a media goal.

Good objectives will also be quantifiable. It is easy to say that you wish to increase sales. Then, if this year you sell 3,000,000 items, you will have met your goal if next year you sell 3,000,001. But is that a real increase? It is more helpful to state quantifiable terms. Say, "Next year, we will increase our sales by 2.2 percent" or "Next year, we will increase sales by 60,000 units." Then you will know for sure whether you have increased your sales, and you will know for sure whether you have met your goal.

Consistency with Message Strategies

It is also important for your media goals and objectives to be consistent with other goals and objectives, as well as with other strategies. We have already seen that advertising media goals must be consistent with marketing and advertising goals.

Your advertising media goals must also be consistent with strategies from other aspects of the campaign, especially with message strategies. If, for example, the copy and art teams have already decided that they must utilize demonstration to make the advertising campaign effective, then the media goals must reflect the need for media that allow for demonstration. Such media include television and cinema, but it is too early to state what media type will be used; in the goal-setting stage, it is enough to state that the eventual media selection must include media that permit ease of demonstration.

There has long been a controversy over which should be decided first,

Exhibit 5.2

Examples of Marketing, Advertising, and Media Objectives

Here are examples of categories that might be used for objectives in marketing, advertising, and media.

Marketing objectives	Advertising objectives	Media objectives
Sales levels (in dollars and in units)	Merchandising support	Efficiency
	Creative considerations	CPP and CPM—
Sales shares (in percentages and in competitive indices)	Media considerations:	Then, TAI and GRP targets can be
	Flexibility	derived
	Contingency	Reach
Product position	Timing:	Frequency
Geographic distribution	Flights	Impact
General consumer profile	Hiatus periods	Continuity
Competitive goal	Sustaining periods	Targets:
Timing during year	Budget considerations:	Groups
Timing by seasons	Allocations to:	Regions
Packaging	Regions	Markets
Pricing	Markets	Audiences
Types of store or other outlets	Media functions	Creative considerations and support
	Targets	Media capabilities
Relative needs for awareness, knowledge, interest, desire and sales	Target markets:[a]	Flexibility
	Areas or regions	Merchandising support
	Target groups[a]	Competitive strategies
	Target audiences[a]	Circulation numbers
Distribution	Levels of awareness, knowledge, preference, desire, and purchase	Audience sizes[b]
		Matched with prospects numbers
	Competitive considerations	Media mix vs. media concentration[c]
	Show package?	Advertising units
	Tell price?	Coupons

[a]Target markets, target groups, and target audiences are often left to the strategy stage, rather than included as objectives.
[b]All given in audience terms, not simply in demographics.
[c] Note that media types to be used are usually considered strategies rather than objectives.

the advertising message or the advertising media. It makes sense for media to come first, because it would be silly and wasteful for the message and creative strategies to develop messages for, say, billboards if outdoor advertising is not included in the schedule. In fact, most often message dictates media. If the creative, message, or copy staff needs certain capabilities, it is usually up to the media goals and plans to accommodate them. In the best case, both media and message will be developed alongside each other, simultaneously, so that each can draw upon the expertise and capabilities of the other. Because of the time constraints involved in advertising, however, this ideal situation too often does not occur.

Marketing Goals Bring Media Plans

So there you have the outline of how to establish goals and objectives, whether for marketing, advertising, media, or any other phase of the marketing effort. You also have an understanding of the process: first, goals and objectives, then strategies, and finally tactics. And you can see how the various phases must work together and support each other.

Good objectives and goals are essential in every phase of your work, and advertising media work is no exception.

In some cases, the campaign targets are established as part of the goals and objectives, but more often, targets are part of the strategies. In the next chapter, you will learn more about setting up and reaching your advertising media targets.

Chapter 6

Defining the Target Audience

Nothing is more important in building an effective media plan than properly defining the target audience. An efficient execution of an improperly targeted media plan is not going to matter. As brand manager, you need to ensure that the media plan and the creative execution are working together. If the agency's creative group is crafting commercials for an upscale, suburban soccer mom while the media group is working on an efficient media plan aimed at a downscale, rural, single mom, then your advertising program is likely to be ineffective and maybe even offensive.

The term *target* can have a wide variety of uses and meanings. A *target market* typically refers to the geographic market you are considering for your advertising. Some advertisers use the term *target group* to define a demographic target, while others use *target audience* to mean just the media target. In this chapter, we will be using the term *target audience* to mean the media audience.

Arriving at the right target audience appears on the surface to be a simple exercise, but it takes careful crafting and tremendous coordination to get the most out of your marketing budget. The target you choose must make sense from a business perspective, a marketing perspective, a media perspective, and a creative perspective. Unless all your stars are aligned, your spaceship will likely hit an asteroid.

For example, in the late 1990s, Chef Boyardee changed its target emphasis to talk to teen boys, who were the largest consumer of the brand. Message strategy was crafted and tested for teen boys. A media plan was fully developed for teen boys. The program resulted in a double-digit decline in brand sales for Chef Boyardee. But doesn't targeting your best consumers make sense? The answer is, only if they are buying the product. In this case, mom still bought the brand and, while kids were the ultimate consumers, mom was still making the purchase decision. When the target was subsequently changed to favor mothers, brand sales began to rise. The moral is that you must start with the right objectives before moving toward a proper target.

Start with the Right Objectives

Isn't getting the proper target as simple as finding out who is using the brand and getting your message to them? As we saw in the Chef Boyardee situation, teen boys may be the consumption target, but they are rarely near a grocery store to buy the product. Obviously, understanding who uses your brand is paramount to the targeting process, but it is not the best place to begin.

The place to begin to define the target is with the behavior you want to change. This behavior may be included in the creative brief but is many times left out of the media discussion. For example, you may have a marketing objective of increasing the user base of your brand. You need to attract new users. If your media plan targets heavy users of the brand, are you going to meet that goal? Of course not.

It is important to outline the specific objective that your marketing plan seeks to accomplish before evaluating the appropriate media target. As we will see, the media planning group should be right in the midst of defining the target, but it is more than strictly a media exercise.

Let's take a look at the soup category. Campbell's soup dominates the U.S. market, so the company must try to expand the category in order to attain growth. Campbell's can do this either by getting more people to eat soup or by getting current users to use it more frequently in recipes. Brands such as Progresso and Healthy Choice need current soup users to switch to their brands. Other brands, such as Lipton and Knorr, look for niche markets: Lipton wants people who will cook with dry soup, and Knorr wants people who rarely if ever use prepared soups.

As brand manager, you need to assess the strengths and weaknesses of the brand in question. If your charge is to grow the brand by 5 percent, then you have a number of ways to get there.

One of the most likely ways to accomplish this goal is to get your current users to use your brand more often. In this case, you would target your current user base. You may also have to attract new users to the brand, either from other brands (stealing share) or by growing the category. This would lead to a target that may not necessarily be your brand's existing audience. Perhaps there is an ethnic niche that hasn't been mined. Or there may be a purchase influence dynamic at play, where the influencer drives the business, rather than the actual purchaser.

Again, all your goals must align. Start with the business goal, which is typically growing the business at X percent. Then ask yourself how you are going to get there. From this point, you should assess your brand versus the category and the competition. Is the product category growing at the same rate as the brand? Is there a gap between your brand and the category that could lead to a potential source of business? Or is there some sort of competitive threat or opportunity that would lead to a growth opportunity for the brand? Once these issues are raised with both the agency and the brand group, you can begin to define the proper target audience.

Tools for Defining the Target Audience

A number of secondary research tools can aid in defining the media target. Over the years, there have been a number of improvements in linking actual brand purchase data to media behavior. These have led to a recent rise in the ability to model schedules and determine the sales impact potential of various media alternatives.

Historically, the two nationally syndicated research studies used by media planners were Mediamark Research Inc. (MRI) and Simmons Market Research Bureau. Both annual studies were initially designed to support the magazine industry with sales and audience data. MRI has now become the standard for most brand media planning, while Simmons has moved into the custom research arena. Simmons recently teamed up with MasterCard to offer brand purchase data on an aggregate basis—a very powerful tool for goods that are not tracked by panel data from the Nielsen Company or Information Resources, Inc. (IRI) InfoScan. Nielsen and IRI are the two services that track manufacturers' brand movements through grocery store chains. Both have powerful databases of purchase behavior that are used to understand the purchase dynamics of a multitude of brands and categories.

MRI is currently the preferred national media planning tool. It provides information on more than 500 categories and 6,000 brands. MRI is the most widely used syndicated research service for determining magazine readership, measuring 235 titles using a "recent reading" technique with logo cards and a "sort board," with which respondents sort logos based on their reading habits of the past month. MRI also collects information on television, cable, radio networks and formats, newspaper readership, and Internet usage.

MRI's sample is 26,000 adults age 18 and older (18+), so it is highly reliable. MRI surveys twice a year, so most media planners use the MRI Doublebase, which has 50,000 respondents as the key media targeting tool. The Doublebase is linked to other segmentation schemes such as PRIZM (Claritas' market segmentation system), Spectra, and NPD, which have developed consumer segmentation analyses that divide the population into common groups based on geography, demographics, and purchase behaviors. A typical segmentation study may have as many as 60 discrete groups. This brings us to the second major media planning tool—one used in the packaged-goods industry.

Nielsen and Spectra have developed a tool that bridges the gap between retail tracking and consumer targeting. This tool connects actual product purchase behavior with Spectra's lifestyle segmentation. Spectra's lifestyle segmentation grid allows the brand manager to analyze consumer behavior not only for media but for consumer promotion as well. With this segmentation scheme becoming very popular for brands, Spectra has become much more important in the media planning process with its link to MRI data.

Using this system, the media planner can get actual brand purchase data that can be linked to media behavior. Until this time, media planners used MRI for both media and marketing data. Now media planners can confirm MRI marketing data and use the same MRI data for media planning.

The Simmons National Consumer Survey (NCS) is another brand planning tool that is particularly powerful in the retail sector. It offers much the same data as MRI but is more extensive in terms of its own segmentation schemes. It is also a nice double-check for media planners to use in conjunction with MRI.

There are two local market tools available primarily for local retail planning. Scarborough Research, a service in joint partnership with the Nielsen Company and Arbitron, Inc., measures local media markets for the leading 75 U.S. markets. The Media Audit is a competitive product that offers a much deeper market list at 86 markets but not quite the level of detail in terms of advertisers measured. Both are excellent sources for analyzing local market activity and can be manipulated to include custom regions.

Those are the key secondary resources used in broad-based media planning. Once a plan is developed, media buyers use specific audience measurement tools for negotiation purposes. The key broadcast sources are Nielsen for television and cable and Arbitron for radio. Recently, there has been a move toward primary research studies for the brand that can be geocoded by either a PRIZM or Spectra database and linked back to other studies such as MRI.

The Heavy-User Definition

Now that you have the right tools, how do you go about defining an audience? There are a number of ways to look at the audience. We have identified some of these from the marketing objectives. An important way to look at your audience profile is in terms of consumption.

The Pareto principle states that 20 percent of the audience represents 80 percent of the consumption. There is a heavy-user segment for nearly every brand. The heavy user may not represent 80 percent of consumption, but there is usually a strong ratio that is typically in the 2-to-1 range for usage-to-users ratios. Looking at the heavy, medium, and light users of a brand is an excellent analysis tool and a viable way to target (See Tables 6.1 and 6.2).

Table 6.1

Tomato Sauce Category Usage Analysis

Sauce category range	Users (000)	%	Volume (000)	%	Avg.
Heavy 6+	3,587	17	40,030	50	11.2
Medium 3–5	5,892	28	22,208	28	3.8
Light 1–2	11,395	55	17,359	22	1.5
	20,874	100	79,597	100	3.8

Source: 2001 MRI Doublebase.

Table 6.2

Diced Tomato Category Usage Analysis

Diced category range	Users (000)	%	Volume (000)	%	Avg.
Heavy 6+	1,867	14	15,406	41	80.0
Medium 3–5	2,481	18	8,487	22	3.4
Light 1–2	9,456	69	13,970	37	1.5
	13,804	100	37,863	100	2.7

Source: 2001 MRI Doublebase.

Let's look at Hunt's tomato sauce. Here, the heavy user for tomato sauce represents 17 percent of the user base but accounts for 50 percent of the users. This might suggest that Hunt's must not lose the heavy-user group because it is a small yet vital part of the category. However, the real opportunity may be to target those other 83 percent of the users to get them to use the brand more often.

You can extend the heavy-user analysis to look for gaps between how your brand attracts users and how the category attracts users. In this Hunt's example, suppose that the category of heavy users is concentrated in the age cell of 25 to 34, while Hunt's heavy users are in the age cell 35 to 49. This means that Hunt's has an opportunity to grow the brand by attacking this usage gap.

Another gap to analyze is the one that exists between competitive brands. For example, there is a definite difference in usage between Hunt's and its major competitor, Del Monte. After assessing why this difference exists, the brand can determine if this gap is something that advertising can impact or if it is the result of a product trait.

The heavy-user concept is certainly one that packaged-goods brand managers use on a regular basis. However, retail and business-to-business brand managers can use this theory as well to segment their audience.

For example, a grocery retailer knows that a mom with kids is likely to spend more on groceries than a single retired adult. The grocery retailer may use basket size (how many products and subsequently dollars a person is buying from the store) as a barometer of a heavy user. So, a shopper who spends $200 on an average visit is worth more than the one who spends $50 per visit. With sophisticated retail databases so prevalent in today's retail landscape, this type of analysis is relatively easy to conduct.

In the business-to-business world, transactions aren't usually as frequent as in retail or packaged goods. However, there is still a size dimension that relates to heavy usage. One way that business-to-business marketers can evaluate their sales database is to see how large the sales are in rank order or to have their financial department help them assess the profitability of each customer in terms of sales versus customer support required to service that customer. Each of these methods can be used to arrive at some form of ranking of heavy to light usage or profitable to less profitable customer.

Lifestyle and Lifestage Segmentation

Beyond the usage method of targeting, there are a number of lifestyles and lifestage assessment methods that affect media targeting. It is possible to gain insight into your target audience by looking at their lifestyles lifestage. We noted that the key tools for assessing lifestyle and lifestage are PRIZM and Spectra. Both of these research tools define lifestyle largely by where you live and how affluent you are. For example, the lifestyle of a consumer who lives in an upscale suburb is very different from that of a consumer living in a downscale urban area. This type of analysis helps put a face on your target and may suggest that you need differing media approaches to reach various lifestyle groups.

Another way to look at your target group is by their lifestage. Consumer patterns of behavior are sometimes dictated by where you are in your life. There is a huge difference between a 25-year-old mother of two and a 25-year-old working woman with no kids. In many cases, lifestages serve as marketing milestones that require different media approaches. For example, if you are a senior in college, it is likely that credit card companies have been soliciting you, since they know you will be getting a job soon and establishing credit. Similarly, new parents receive all sorts of coupons for various baby products as well as banking products to save for their children's education.

Table 6.3

PAM Cooking Spray

	Lifestage						
Spectra lifestyle	18–34 w/kids	18–34 w/o kids	35–54 w/kids	35–54 w/o kids	55–64	65	Total lifestyle
Upscale suburbs	105	53	112	104	136	154	116
Traditional families	73	55	93	107	130	178	111
Mid/upscale suburbs	62	60	108	82	122	142	108
Metro elite	78	34	88	71	121	130	83
Working-class towns	77	45	94	86	145	157	104
Rural towns and farms	48	44	86	103	127	145	99
Mid-urban melting pot	48	38	83	73	108	148	89
Downscale rural	49	35	90	86	119	162	103
Downscale urban	56	30	85	71	97	148	87
Total	65	42	94	87	124	151	100

Sources: AC Nielsen and Spectra/Media*PLAN*. Reprinted with permission.

Let's look at example of lifestyle and lifestage for users of PAM Cooking Spray (Table 6.3). The PAM brand attracts an older and more affluent audience. The challenge for PAM brand is to generate a new base of users with a younger audience.

Generations as a Target

We have discussed various demographic and brand usage approaches to targeting. One other method of targeting is to find common ground among various generations of consumers. Generations are brief periods of time that are connected with popular culture. Consumers of the same generation are connected not only by age but by the various milestones they have reached together. Some unifying characteristics include music, fads, inventions, politics, and social movements. For example, the 1960s ushered in the British Invasion of rock stars to the United States, led by the Beatles. World War II colored two generations: The first has been termed the G.I. Generation because its members fought in the war as adults; these Americans were later referred to as the "Greatest Generation" for defeating the Axis of Evil. The second generation impacted included those who were children during WWII; dubbed the Silent Generation, these Americans grew up in families that were pre-occupied with the war. Table 6.4 offers a list of U.S. generations for the past 100 years.

Generations can be a very important method of targeting, since these

Table 6.4

List of U.S. Generations

Generation	Born	Notable Occurrences
Lost Generation	1883–1910	• Experienced WWI
G.I. Generation	1911–1924	• Fought WWII as adults
		• Called the "Greatest Generation"
Silent Generation	1925–1942	• Repressed childhoods due to WWII
Boomer Generation	1943–1965	• Civil Rights movement
		• Woodstock
Generation X	1965–1985	• Rise of mass media
		• End of Cold War
		• MTV
Generation Y	1986–2001	• Rise of Information Age
		• Internet
Generation Z	2002–	• Unknown

groups are connected not only demographically but also emotionally and historically. Many times, an advertiser will use music or images that stir emotions within various groups. From a media perspective, it is important to be sensitive to the demographic nuances of generations as well as to patterns of culture that may be a good forum to deliver an advertising message.

Behavioral Targeting

Another way to target your market is by how its members behave. This type of targeting is very popular in the online world, since it is possible to track the Web sites someone is visiting on a real-time basis. For example, if you have just visited a Web site on border collies, you are likely to be a pet owner and receptive to a new dog food brand. That is how behavioral targeting works in the online world. But this type of targeting is not exclusive to this space. You can target people who drive Corvettes. Or you can target men who play golf. The idea of behavioral targeting is to have a relevant message for someone when it is most relevant to them—that is, when they are actually demonstrating or behaving in a way that would indicate that your brand is important to them.

This type of targeting can be stretched to more than just activities. You might consider targeting bargain hunters, those people who clip coupons or visit Web sites that sell discounted goods. In this way, you are finding some behavior outside of the brand's purchase dynamics that might be a good fit for the audience.

Purchaser vs. Influencer

So far we have talked about the brand in terms of who is buying the product. For packaged goods, this is typically the mother in a household. But she is not always the one consuming the products. While our secondary research tools do an excellent job of defining the purchaser, they do not necessarily define the actual consumer of the product.

To understand this dynamic, the brand needs to do primary research to understand whether or not there are influences that tip the scale beyond the actual purchaser of the product. For many items, the child in the household exerts the brand influence. Many households purchase private-label cereal and put that cereal in the branded box so children will think it is from their favorite branded source.

In James McNeal's book *The Kids Market: Myths and Realities,* the author offers estimates of children's influence on parents' spending for various items. These items range from those where you might guess the children's influence would be high, such as toys, candy, and video games, to items where children have smaller influences, such as sporting goods, sunglasses, and salad dressing (See Table 6.5).

The challenge for the brand manager and the media group is to determine how to balance these influences. In the case of cereal, do you target mothers or do you target only the children? Of course, you would like to do both, but if you do not have enough funds, which one do you pick? Or should you blend the funds in a ratio, say 70 percent for mothers and 30 percent for children? These issues certainly need to be resolved before the media plan can be fully developed.

The issue of purchase influence is not confined to mothers and children. Many household purchases from the family car to the house to vacations are made with varying degrees of influence from both heads of the household. Recent trends in health care show that adult children assert influence over their now-senior parents. So the issue of purchase influence is very far reaching and can be the key decision in the media targeting process.

Other Brand Influencers

The issue of brand influence is not just the domain of brand purchaser versus brand user. In the retail and service area, the employee is a huge influence on the delivery of a service and the key to customer satisfaction. As a result, a retailer or service brand manager often makes sure that the employees are a media target for the advertising.

Sometimes retail or service advertising is based around a consumer

Table 6.5

Estimates of Children's Influence on Selected Product Purchases

Selected products	Industry sales (billion $)	Influence (percent)	Influence (billion $)
Amusement parks	5.0	45	2.3
Athletic shoes	5.6	20	1.1
Autos	221.7	8	17.7
Bakery goods	26.1	10	2.6
Baking mixes/dough	2.8	15	0.4
Bar soaps	1.5	20	0.3
Batteries	3.5	25	0.9
Beauty aids (kids)	1.2	70	0.8
Bicycles	2.9	40	1.2
Blank audio cassettes	0.4	15	0.1
Bottled water	2.0	9	0.2
Bread	13.0	20	2.6
Cameras (still) and film	4.6	12	0.5
Candy and gum	19.0	35	6.7
Canned pasta	0.6	60	0.3
Casual dining	21.0	30	6.3
Cereal, hot	0.7	27	0.2
Cereal, cold	8.0	50	4.0
Clothing (kids)	18.4	70	12.9
Condiments	5.0	10	0.5
Consumer electronics	36.0	12	4.3
Cookies	5.4	40	2.2
Costume jewelry	4.0	12	0.5
Dairy goods	40.2	12	4.8
Deli goods	11.1	9	1.0
Eye ware	13.5	10	1.4
Fast foods	89.8	35	31.4
Fragrances (kids)	0.3	70	0.2
Frozen breakfasts	0.6	15	0.1
Frozen dinners	4.0	15	0.6
Frozen novelties	1.5	75	1.1
Frozen sandwiches	0.3	30	0.1
Fruit snacks	0.4	80	0.3
Fruits and vegetables, canned	3.0	20	0.6
Fruits and vegetables, fresh	52.1	8	4.2
Furniture, furnishings (kids)	5.0	35	1.8
Greeting cards	6.2	15	0.9
Hair care	3.8	10	0.4
Hobby items	1.0	40	0.4

Table 6.5 *(continued)*

Selected products	Industry sales (billion $)	Influence (percent)	Influence (billion $)
Home computers	4.5	18	0.8
Hotels, mid-price	5.5	12	0.7
Ice cream	8.7	25	2.2
Isotonic drinks	1.0	15	0.2
Jellies and jams	2.6	23	0.6
Juices and juice drinks	11.8	33	3.9
Meats, fresh	43.1	12	5.2
Meats, packaged	17.1	18	3.1
Microwave foods	2.3	30	0.7
Movies	1.6	30	0.5
Over-the-counter drugs	11.0	12	1.3
Peanut butter	1.4	40	0.6
Pet foods	8.2	12	1.0
Pet supplies	3.7	12	0.4
Pizza, frozen	0.9	40	0.4
Pudding and gelatin	0.9	25	0.2
Recorded music	3.4	22	0.7
Refrigerated puddings	0.2	20	0.0
Salad dressing	3.0	10	0.3
Salty snacks	13.6	25	3.4
School supplies	2.3	35	0.8
Seafood	8.0	15	1.2
Shoes (kids)	2.0	50	1.0
Soda	58.0	30	17.4
Software, learning	1.3	50	0.7
Soup	3.0	20	0.6
Sporting goods	30.0	15	4.5
Spreadable cheese	0.3	20	0.1
Sunglasses	2.0	10	0.2
Toaster products	0.3	45	0.1
Toothpaste	1.5	20	0.3
Toys	14.0	70	9.8
Video games	6.0	60	3.6
Video rentals	11.0	25	2.8
Wristwatches	5.9	12	0.7
Yogurt	1.6	12	0.2
Total	$932.7		$187.7

Source: James McNeal, *The Kids Market: Myths and Realities* (Ithaca, NY: Paramount Market Publishing).

promise that employees must fulfill. For example, a grocery chain ran a promotion that if you weren't checked out within five minutes, they would give a discount off their groceries. To ensure that the employees were up for the challenge, the marketing manager ran an advertising campaign saluting the great employees of the store. This campaign led to a big increase in store pride by the employees, so when the promotion hit, they were more than ready to execute it.

The world of business-to-business marketing has a very complicated set of influences. Since the purchase of a business item doesn't involve your own money, it comes with an entirely different dynamic. For example, when a company buys a computer, the user of the computer wants something that they are comfortable with; the IT group wants something that fits into their overall IT framework; the finance group wants to minimize costs; and the CEO wants the greatest productivity. All of these customers have influence over the purchase. In many cases, however, the actual purchaser (the person who writes the check) has the least amount of influence over the purchase.

So, as a business-to-business brand manager, it is important to walk the advertising agency and the media group through the sales process so that they understand its various components.

Growing Ethnic Diversity

In the golden age of television, the media target was fairly easy to discern. Take a look at *Leave It to Beaver,* and you had your audience. It consisted of a Caucasian family with a working husband, a stay-at-home mom, and two kids. Of course, that was 1960. The times have changed a lot since then.

Everyone knows that more women now work than stay at home, although that figure has topped out at about 60 percent, according to the latest U.S. Census Bureau data. The larger trend in the United States is the ethnic diversity of the population. There are many large markets, such as Los Angeles and Miami, where whites are not the majority. The most rapid growth in the population is coming from Hispanic and Asian populations, followed by African Americans.

Obviously, these growth patterns have a lot of bearing on media planning and targeting. Ethnic audiences do watch, listen to, and read media that would be considered general-market media. However, each ethnic group also uses specific media that are tailored to its specific culture. The media planning dilemma is to determine when additional resources should be funneled into ethnic media.

There are two schools of thought on this issue. The first is to determine what percent of the ethnic population is *underdelivered* by the general market media and then to make up that difference in ethnic media. For example, if you were targeting beer-drinking men, you might schedule a commercial on *Monday Night Football*. If *MNF* delivers a 12 rating for all men but only an 8 rating for Hispanic men, there is a 33 percent shortfall for Hispanic men. You can either accept this shortfall or look for programming that will balance the delivery for Hispanic men. Assessing underdelivery of various target groups is an excellent media analysis. This example would suggest that the current buy of *Monday Night Football* may not be enough if Hispanic men are a key part of your target.

This brings us to the second school of thought, which is marketing versus media. If Hispanic men are a crucial target audience, then you should market to them. Scheduling support in ethnic media is as much a political statement as it is a method of reaching the right audience. It means that you recognize the importance of this group, and that has an impact well beyond the standard media analysis.

It is important in ethnic markets to understand the media impact of the plan in terms of media delivery. If an ethnic segment is growing and is important, then develop a marketing program to cultivate that group. That is where the brand manager and the media team need to work together to ensure that all aspects of strategic thought are represented before proceeding.

Economic Impact of Targeting

We have looked at media targeting from the perspective of who is the best audience to reach in order to make your business grow. There are also economic implications of targeting. Each decision you make on defining your target audience will have an effect on the cost of media. Thus, assessing the cost impact of your target decision is important in finalizing your target audience.

In your analysis of various target segments, each one will consume media in different ways. This consumption will lead to various cost trade-offs as you finalize your target audience. For example, research indicates that women watch more television than men. Therefore, it costs more to reach the same number of men through television than it does women. Suppose you decide that it is important to reach both men and women based on the purchase influence dynamics of the brand. If you change the target audience for the media plan from women to adults, you raise your costs by more than 10 percent. Why? You are paying a premium to reach men.

This same dynamic holds true for age. Older adults watch more television than younger adults. It costs dramatically more on a cost-per-rating-point basis to reach adults age 18 to 34 than adults age 55 and over. If you change

Table 6.6

Media CPM Efficiencies Based on Target Size

Target	TV	Cable	Radio	Newspaper	Magazines	OOH	Online
Broad Target	*****	2	*	*****	*****	5	1
	****	2	**	****	****	4	2
	***	3	***	***	***	3	3
	**	4	****	**	****	2	4
Niche Target	*	5	*****	*	*****	1	5
CPM Scale	*****		Highly Efficient				
	*		Not Efficient				

your target from the 18–49 group to the 18–34 group for a television plan, you will have to pay another 5 to 10 percent in costs.

The harder the group is to reach, the more it costs to reach them, which seems like a pretty basic axiom. The curve ball here is that some media are designed to reach a very narrow audience rather than a broad one. This axiom holds true for the regular television networks, but it does not necessarily apply to cable, where programming is very specific. [See Table 6.6.]

Television and newspapers are very much alike: the broader the audience, the lower the cost to reach them. Radio is just the opposite. Radio formats are tailored for narrow age cells. Each station is trying to own a key demographic. On radio, the tighter the audience, the lower the cost. For example, if you are targeting all men with a radio buy, you would likely need to purchase a news station for the older men and a rock station for the younger men. If you are just targeting young men, you could cut the news and reduce your costs considerably.

Magazines have similar dynamics. There are broad-reach publications, such as *Time, Sports Illustrated,* and *Good Housekeeping.* However, if you are targeting just people who like spicy food, you might be better off with *Chili Pepper* magazine.

The Internet is cut from the same cloth as magazines, with large search engines as the broad-reach vehicles and individual sites as niche properties.

The other economic implications of targeting involve your media budget. If you are like most brand managers, you usually do not have enough resources to do what you want to do. Every brand is under pressure to deliver profits, and media support is one of the easiest budget cuts because it is one of the variable expenses.

If you are faced with marketing a national cereal brand with only $3 million for advertising, yet the competition spends $15 million, you have some tough challenges. Your $3 million will not go far against a broad "mothers" target, but it is certainly enough to generate some noise in the children's market. Or you may want to tackle an ethnic market with your limited budget. Therefore, working with the media-planning group to understand the cost impact dynamics of a target is important.

The target audience is the cornerstone of the media plan. Defining the proper target is crucial for success. It begins with setting the right objectives and then using the tools at your disposal to better identify the audience. Once you have weighed your options from both opportunity and economic perspectives, you are ready to finalize this aspect of the media plan.

Chapter 7
Geography's Role in Planning

Where your product is marketed is as important as to whom your product is marketed. Whether your brand is international or only in the corner grocery store, the role of geography is an important strategic issue when it comes to media planning. How you define where you want to advertise and how much weight you give to one market versus another are key elements in resource usage decisions.

Geography ties in to the target audience definition. As mentioned in chapter 6, PRIZM or Spectra data can be mapped to provide a look at regional pockets of strength or weakness for a brand's target market. Then, as the brand manager, you can decide whether to support geography that has a high concentration of customers or to go fishing for new customers.

Before we get into geographic analysis and the impact of geography on media costs and media vehicle selection, we first need to define our geography.

How to Define Geography

You, the brand manager, tell the media planning group that you want to "heavy-up" (or apply more advertising weight to) Birmingham, Alabama. The media planning group walks away thinking that you want to advertise in the Birmingham designated marketing area (DMA), while you think that the media planning group is looking at the Birmingham Information Resources, Inc. (IRI's) InfoScan market, which consists of seven different DMAs (See Table 7.1).

Obviously, you have a problem. One of the most common problems a brand manager faces is matching up marketing areas to media planning geography. While this sounds fundamental, it is a crucial area that is often overlooked until it is too late, or until a critical mistake is made.

The media planner will usually define geography with the television DMA from Nielsen. A DMA is a group of counties that get the majority of

Table 7.1

IRI (InfoScan) Market to Nielsen Designated Market Area

INFOSCAN Market (ISM): Birmingham, AL

DMA	InfoScan market coverage	
	TVHH (000)	% of ISM
Birmingham	530.7	39.7
Huntsville–Decatur, Florence	317.8	23.7
Montgomery	211.2	15.8
Mobile/Pensacola	117.4	8.8
Tuscaloosa	59.4	4.4
Columbus, GA	50.7	3.8
Anniston	43.2	3.2
Other spill	7.8	0.6
Total	1,338.1	100.0

Source: IRI (InfoScan).

their television viewing from the same home market. There are 210 DMAs in the Nielsen television system. DMAs are fairly static but changes can occur. For example, at different times, Sarasota, Florida, has been its own DMA and has also been a part of the Tampa/St. Petersburg DMA, depending upon how strongly its local station has performed in its home market. Although counties may shift from one DMA to another, DMAs are fairly consistent from year to year.

A second geography used by media planners is the metropolitan statistical area (MSA). An MSA is a census area around a central metropolitan area, as designated by the government. Each MSA comprises a certain number of counties and is smaller than a DMA. Radio stations typically use the MSA as their geography for their signal strength. Some brands use the MSA as their trading area, because a considerable amount of census data exist that can be used to analyze this area. There are approximately 280 MSAs in the United States.

Packaged-goods marketers use either Nielsen panel data or IRI data to analyze sales information. Each of these sources uses broader marketing areas than either a DMA or an MSA. To describe their geography, Nielsen and IRI use approximately 60 market areas, which incorporate the 210 DMAs.

Regardless of the source you are using, it is important to match up these market areas with DMAs before proceeding into media planning. Thus, when you say "Birmingham," you will get all the DMAs in the area and not just the 40 percent of the total marketing area that lies in the Birmingham DMA.

Table 7.2

Georgia Trading Area Analysis: BoJangles Chicken

Zip Code	# Households	Sales	% Total	Sales per HH
30327	4,760	$150,000	10%	$31.51
33110	5,110	$135,000	9%	$26.42
32112	4,210	$120,000	8%	$28.50
35333	4,510	$120,000	8%	$26.60
30353	5,010	$105,000	7%	$20.96
32121	4,420	$105,000	7%	$23.76
31760	4,130	$90,000	6%	$21.79
32211	4,610	$90,000	6%	$19.52
30761	4,750	$75,000	5%	$15.80
34276	5,000	$60,000	4%	$12.00
Top 10 Total	46,510			
All Others	54,000	$450,000	30%	$8.33
Total	100,510	$1,500,000	100%	$14.92

If you are a brand manager of a retail chain, then you define your market by the store's trading area. A trading area is a geographic area based on where your customers actually live or work. For example, most fast-food restaurants use a three-mile trading radius as their standard for defining their individual store's trading area. Other retail stores may draw from a wider area, but most retailers have a specific part of the market that comprises the majority of their customers. To market effectively to this group, a retail brand manager conducts a trade area analysis. This is usually done by evaluating the point-of-sale system used by retailers to capture customer names and addresses. The above chart shows a zip code analysis for a fast food chicken restaurant in Georgia.

As Table 7.2 shows, a concentration of sales comes from just a few zip codes. This provides the media planner with information to make an intelligent decision on a variety of media. Perhaps there is a billboard location that makes sense in this area. Or there may be a need to provide inserts or direct mail with coupon offers to area residents.

Geography can play a role in business-to-business marketing as well. The difference in business marketing compared to consumer marketing is that the decision process can occur in more than one market. For example, a cellular phone company that markets to the offshore oil industry found that the users of their service lived in rural markets near the coasts of Louisiana and Texas; however, the decision makers working on the oil rigs with the workers lived in more urban markets such as Houston, New Orleans, and Baton Rouge. In addition, the headquarters for most oil companies were in a western suburban area of Houston, more than 100 miles from the coast.

In this case, the brand manager had to develop a different strategy for users of the service versus corporate headquarters.

So, any goods or services will have geographical influences, whether they are national, on a local market basis, or even as micro as a city block. Regardless of your brand's situation, the same discipline and tools should be used to determine the appropriate geographical media approach.

How to Analyze Geography

Now that everyone is working with the same definitions, it is time to analyze your sales by geography to determine strengths and weaknesses. The classic method is to develop a BDI/CDI analysis.

BDI stands for *brand development index,* which tells how strong a market's sales are in relation to its population size. This index is the percentage of your brand's sales compared to the percent of the population in a certain market. Suppose you have 3.4 percent of your sales in Dallas, a city that represents 1.7 percent of the population of the United States. The BDI would be 200 for your brand ($3.4 \div 1.7 \times 100$).

An index of 100 means the brand sales in that market mirror the population. If the index is less than 100, then the brand is not consumed up to the per capita level; if the BDI is over 100, consumption is greater than the per capita level.

CDI stands for *category development index.* Just like a BDI, a CDI is the percent of category sales compared to the percent of the population. You use the CDI as a measure of potential, while the BDI is a measure of actual brand strength.

The best way to look at a BDI/CDI analysis is to graph it in a quadrant chart. Exhibit 7.1 shows a quadrant chart with each grid reflecting a different relationship between the brand and the category. In quadrant I, both the brand and category are strong. This is a good area to defend. Quadrant II shows that the BDI is much stronger than the CDI, which means that the only brand growth here would be limited to growing the category. In quadrant III, the category is stronger than the brand. This is the area of opportunity. And quadrant IV shows that both the brand and category are weak. This is an area to avoid spending advertising dollars.

One last analysis is to create your own *brand opportunity index* (BOI). This is done by dividing the CDI by the BDI. For example, you have a brand where Atlanta has a CDI of 120 but a BDI of 80. That would correspond to a BOI of 150 ($120 \div 80$). This market represents a very high growth possibility for the brand. On the other hand, if Orlando has a CDI of 120 but a BDI of 150, then the BOI of 80 ($120 \div 150$) might make it less attractive as

Exhibit 7.1

Brand Opportunities Analysis

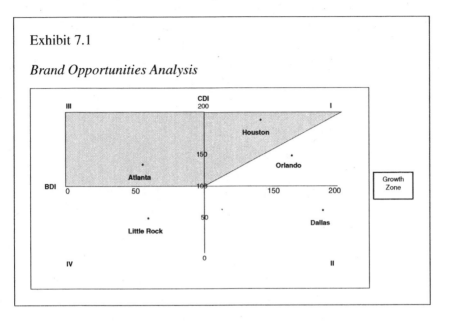

a growth market than Atlanta, even though both the BDI and CDI would put Orlando in the top quadrant (See Table 7.3). Both Nielsen and IRI research show that advertising has the best opportunity to "grow" a brand where it has a strong BOI. So, once you calculate your BDI and CDI and put them in a quadrant chart, calculate your BOI for the final opportunity analysis.

The same BDI/CDI analysis can be done in the retail as well as business-to-business arena. In the retail area, you may want to look at BDI/CDI on a market level, not just on a trading area basis. Since the number of stores may determine the strength or weakness of a market, retailers use a sales-per-trading-area analysis to evaluate one store versus another. This can be done by simply calculating the sales of the store and dividing by the number of households within the store's trading area.

Factoring in Distribution

The BDI/CDI analysis is a classic one, but before finalizing your market "heavy-up" decision, you should dig a bit deeper to understand the reason behind the numbers. Suppose that in the Atlanta example, where your BDI is only 80, your brand was in only 50 percent of the available points of distribution. If you adjusted the BDI for the lack of distribution, the BDI would be 160. Now the opportunity market that you thought you had may not be one after all.

Table 7.3

Brand Opportunity Index

DMA	BDI	CDI	BOI
Dallas/Ft. Worth	200	80	40
Atlanta	80	120	150
Houston	150	200	133
Little Rock	90	50	55
Orlando	150	120	80

For packaged-goods products, the term for distribution is *all commodity volume* (ACV). This is a fancy name for the percent of the distribution channel in which the brand is available.

Distribution is an important element when looking at sales by market. Distribution, or the lack thereof, may be one of the reasons why a brand performs the way it does. One way to equalize the effects of spotty distribution is to do a sales-per-distribution-point analysis. This analysis looks at the sales-velocity-per-distribution percentage. It may uncover where a brand is performing well yet has distribution weaknesses. This can be a good tool for the brand manager to use with the sales group to shore up any weaknesses in the distribution area. For example, suppose that your brand has 2 percent of its sales in Dallas/Fort Worth, which has roughly 2 percent of the U.S. population. You would say that Dallas is an average market with a BDI of 100. But if you found that you had your brand in only half the available retail outlets in Dallas, then you would say that Dallas actually has a BDI of 200 in the outlets where your brand is available. Based on this analysis, Dallas looks like a great market, once you gain that crucial missing amount of distribution.

From a media planning perspective, understanding the distribution of the brand is an important facet in selecting either markets to "heavy-up" or test markets. Before just blindly proceeding with the BDI/CDI analysis, step back and ask about the brand's distribution.

Applying Media to Geography

Now that you and your team understand what markets you want to target and are working from the same market definitions, you can begin to analyze what media to apply to various levels of geography.

While most media can be purchased on a national, regional, or local basis, each medium has its geographical nuances. Let's review the major media and how they can be purchased at various geographical levels.

Television air time can be purchased on a DMA basis locally or on a network television basis nationally. The major networks—ABC, CBS, NBC, and Fox—can even offer broad regional coverage based typically on five large regions. The only nuance to network television is using syndicated programming, which is cleared on a local basis. For example, a syndicated program such as *Wheel of Fortune* is actually sold DMA by DMA to a local series of unrelated local stations. In exchange for taking the program, the local station gets a certain amount of commercial inventory to sell, while the syndicator keeps its "national" inventory. Depending upon the syndicator's success, a program might clear all 100 percent of the country or just a portion of it.

Cable television air time can be purchased locally and nationally. Most cable networks do not offer regional opportunities. However, there are regional cable sports networks available to purchase. Cable is a tricky medium from a geographic perspective. Cable channels are purchased by local cable operators. Each cable network is available in various percentages of the cable universe. Popular networks like CNN or the Discovery Channel are in most cable lineups. A niche network like the Food Network may not be in a large number of the cable lineups. While national cable has its set of geographic issues, purchasing cable locally is even more challenging. A local buy must be purchased from individual cable operators in that market. In a market such as Dallas/Fort Worth, that may mean dealing with more than ten different cable companies. This complexity means that executing a local cable buy on a DMA basis can be difficult in some markets.

Radio air time can be purchased locally on an MSA basis or on a national basis. Locally, radio is similar to television, with the only nuance being signal strength. Some stations are stronger than others, which can impact listening on the fringes of the MSA. Network radio is fairly similar to network television and syndication. You can purchase commercials that air on stations across the country, and you can purchase what is called long-form programming that is similar to syndication. *The American Top 40,* a radio countdown of the week's most popular songs, is an example of a long-form program.

Magazine space can be purchased locally, regionally, or nationally. It is possible to purchase space in a magazine such as *Good Housekeeping* on a national basis, or just in the Southeast, or just in the Chicago DMA. The smaller the publication's circulation, the less likely it is that you can purchase space in it on a regional or local basis. Obviously, there are regional and local magazines of every shape, topic, and size available to purchase.

With the exception of *USA Today,* the *Wall Street Journal,* and the national edition of the *New York Times,* newspaper space cannot be purchased on a national basis. However, there are products that come within a newspaper that you can purchase. Free-standing inserts (FSIs) run in the Sunday newspaper and carry a wide variety of coupons. The largest purveyor of FSIs is a company called Valassis. You can create a national, regional, or local buy using these inserts. *Parade* magazine is another vehicle that is distributed in the Sunday newspaper and is purchased like any other magazine space. In addition, newspapers offer the opportunity to market on a micro level, targeting inserts by zip code; insert-only companies such as ADVO provide the same service.

Online advertising can be purchased on any geographic level, including worldwide. A Web portal like AOL offers any level of banner or other program support to the widest or narrowest geography possible. Search engines such as Yahoo! also offer these opportunities.

Out-of-home media—billboards and signs on subways and buses—are, for the most part, a local medium. However, you can buy advertising space on a rolling basis on bus routes that cover much of the country. Beyond these standard out-of-home media, the alternative media such as airplane banners, beach logos, telephone-booth advertisements, and bathroom ads are extremely local.

Economics of Media by Geography

We have had a cursory look at how media can be purchased by various levels of geography. There are economies of scale moving from local to national levels of support. Because each medium is a bit different in its local-versus-national purchase, it is sometimes more efficient to schedule a national advertising placement than to buy a number of markets on a local basis.

The rule of thumb for calculating when network television becomes more cost efficient than buying spot television is when the brand is available in approximately two thirds (66 percent) of the states in the United States. Prime-time and sports programming have the lowest national-to-local break-even point, which is usually at 66 percent. Morning, daytime, and evening news programs can be slightly higher than this level, but the two-thirds rule is a good one to go by.

Because cable is not as efficient as television on a local basis, its national-to-local break-even point is very low. If you are in the top five media markets in the United States, it is less expensive to purchase national advertising than to buy just those five markets. The national-to-local break-even point for cable is around 25 percent of the United States, although it can be even lower if you are comparing some very inefficient local markets.

Table 7.4

National-to-Local Break-even Points

Media	Break-even %
Network TV to spot TV (prime)	66
Network radio (:30) to spot radio (:60)	33
Network cable to local cable	25
National magazine to local edition of national magazine	33

In Table 7.4, we have radio and magazine at similar break-even points; both are at 33 percent of the United States. However, there is a bit of a nuance to the radio analysis. Local radio is typically comprised of 60-second commercial units. Many local radio stations have gone to unit-rate pricing, where it costs the same to purchase a 60- or a 30-second commercial; as a result, 30-second commercial units are becoming less common locally. However, national network radio charges 50 percent of the 60-second commercial rate for a 30-second commercial, making network radio much more likely to have 30-second units. So the break-even point for radio uses a 60-second commercial locally and a 30-second commercial nationally.

Now that you know that it is more efficient to purchase national rather than local advertising for your brand, even if the brand does not have national distribution, should you be concerned that you are advertising where the brand is not available? While this decision can be a double-edged sword, there are certainly more reasons to advertise nationally than not if you have the opportunity.

Beyond the cost implications, national commercials or advertisements get more favorable placement in a given program or publication than local ads; studies have shown that national advertising can have upwards of 25 percent more impact or retention value for your commercial message. From a marketing perspective, this type of advertising can help seed your brand in future expansion areas so you may not have to spend as much once you gain that distribution. In today's retail climate, if you can land distribution in a chain like Wal-Mart, you have a national brand instantly.

Geographical planning is a key element in media planning. The first step in the process is to understand your market-area definitions. From there, you can analyze your brand's strengths and weaknesses. Develop your BDI/CDI analysis. Determine how you are going to treat different market groups. Then look for economies of scale as you roll out your brand nationally.

The next chapter deals with another cornerstone of good media planning: the seasonal issues of brand consumption and media costs.

Chapter 8
Seasonality and Timing

What time of year your advertising runs is a critical factor in your advertising campaign: perhaps timing is not as critical as your target audience or your geographic selection, but proper timing can still make the difference between an effective campaign outcome and a marginal result. The time of the year affects media costs, media effectiveness, and consumers' buying patterns. Nevertheless, there are lots of other advertising media scheduling factors that you must take into account, including schedule flexibility, the pace or rate of advertising, the share of advertising, and possible scheduling remedies for competitive actions.

Seasons and Quarters

Certainly, advertising makes use of the seasons of the year: winter, spring, summer, and fall. But advertising media seasonality refers to a bit more than the four seasons. It also refers to quarters of the year. The first quarter is January through March, the second quarter is April through June, the third quarter is July through September, and the fourth quarter is October through December. However, these quarters do not always line up exactly with the months because there are 52 weeks in the year; a quarter is really 13 weeks long, which does not exactly correspond to any three-month period of time. And because 13 weeks constitutes a quarter of the year, advertising flights, or waves, are often 13 weeks long as well.

The cost and effectiveness of media vary with the time of year, too. Because so much advertising appears during the Christmas shopping season, the fourth quarter has the most advertising—in all media, print as well as broadcast. That means higher levels of competitive advertising during the fourth quarter, which also means that each advertising placement may be less effective during the fourth quarter simply because there are so many competing messages (See Table 8.1). Because of the high demand for advertising during the fourth quarter, the media vehicles may raise their advertising

Table 8.1

Media Effectiveness by Quarters of the Year

Network television	Average household rating			
	1st Qtr	2nd Qtr	3rd Qtr	4th Qtr
Daytime	3.4	3.2	4.1	3.3
Early news	8.0	7.1	6.7	7.8
Prime time	8.8	8.3	6.9	8.8
Late fringe	3.4	3.3	3.2	3.3

Source: Advertising Media Services.

Table 8.2

Advertising Costs by Quarter of the Year

Network television	Average cost per :30 commercial ($)			
	1st Qtr	2nd Qtr	3rd Qtr	4th Qtr
Daytime	18,000	21,000	29,000	21,000
Early news	67,000	73,000	49,000	77,000
Prime time	146,000	160,000	132,000	189,000
Late fringe	49,000	54,000	47,000	53,000

Source: Advertising Media Services.

rates then, too, which can make advertising in the fourth quarter not only less effective, but also more expensive (See Table 8.2).

On the other hand, there is comparatively little advertising in the first quarter, not because it is the beginning of the year, but because it follows the highly used fourth quarter. Many advertisers have expended much of their advertising budgets during the fourth quarter, so they pull back during the first quarter of the following year. Consumers' media usage goes up during the first quarter, however, because bad weather may keep people at home. In broadcast, especially in television, there may also be good programming during the February ratings sweeps, because attractive programs build viewership. So the first quarter may be a bargain for television advertisers: the choice of insertion times is broad because fewer advertisers are trying to buy television advertising time, there are fewer competitive advertisements on the air, and viewership is at one of the year's highest levels.

Other media have seasonal patterns, too. For example, newspaper readership tends to drop during the summer when people go on vacation and suspend their subscriptions. Magazine readership may dwindle during the

Christmas shopping season and then increase after holidays, when the weather is poor for out-of-home activities. Radio usage increases in the summer when school is out. And because the evenings are lighter, people are outside more often than in the winter.

Buying Patterns Affected by the Weather

Consumer purchasing patterns vary during the year, depending on both the product category and the weather. If there is a heavy snowfall at the beginning of winter, consumers may look for snow tires, thinking that it will be a long, snowy winter; if snow falls in March, consumers are less likely to shop for snow tires, figuring that they have already made it through the worst of winter without them. Similarly, a heat wave in May will spur sales of air conditioners, but a heat wave in September may not, again because consumers believe that they have already been through the worst that the season has to offer.

Packaged goods, however, may benefit from weather changes at any time. Whether there is a heat wave in May or September, sales of soft drinks will jump. Nobody will put off a cool drink in September just because most of the summer has already passed. Cold weather in winter typically causes canned soup sales to climb, but hot soup is not nearly as popular during the warm summer months.

Weather can be an important advertising strategy. For example, Quaker Oats ran a campaign based on the theme: "Below 50 degrees is oatmeal weather," and the company worked with the media to trigger the message when the local temperatures fell below 50 degrees.

Day of Week and Time of Day

The season or quarter and the annual climate may affect your media selections and insertions. Similarly, the time of day and the day of the week may be important, too. Golf balls may be advertised on daytime television, but likely only on the weekend. Hair products and packaged food items may do well advertised on weekday daytime television, while lawn fertilizer or health items may do better during the early news or on prime time (roughly 8:00 to 11:00 in the evening).

Other Scheduling Factors

Season, quarter, day, and time are all important, but they may be largely intuitive, and they are among the least complex factors in timing. Several other kinds of timing considerations also come into play in advertising media scheduling, all of importance, yet perhaps not as intuitively obvious.

Susceptibility

Consumers may be more susceptible to a message at certain times. Sylvania focused its advertising for light bulbs on the day when daylight savings time ends and it gets dark earlier. Consumers were more attuned to lights at that time. A classic campaign was conducted for Brinks Security, which ran a radio announcement during work hours that said, "While you are at work, who is watching your home?" These are good examples of exploiting certain times of day, based on consumers' susceptibility.

Flexibility

You may need flexibility in your media buys so you can switch from one media placement to others. Quick tactical maneuvers or other media schedule changes may be needed to meet competitive assaults or to take advantage of such external shifts as economic changes, unusual weather, consumer fads, and real or perceived threats.

When the World Trade Center was brought down by terrorism on September 11, 2001, sales opportunities increased for security products while they decreased for vacation packages. When crime rose on one Caribbean island, that locale developed a serious marketing problem; at the same time, other Caribbean islands gained in tourism as they promoted their safety and security. When Vanilla Coca-Cola became a hit, the opportunity suddenly opened up for other vanilla-flavored foods and beverages. If the economy takes a dip, sales of packaged goods may remain steady, but consumers may switch to smaller packages that require less cash outlay. A longer-than-normal rainy season in spring may delay purchases of lawn weed killers, making it necessary to extend the advertising flights to match; the same can happen with automotive antifreeze when extended warm weather lasts into autumn.

Rate of Advertising

Even your advertising budget may be a scheduling factor. Low levels of advertising are likely to bring low levels of customer response. High levels of advertising, on the other hand, are extremely and sometimes prohibitively expensive.

We have already seen how advertising expenditures can be ameliorated or leveled out by advertising in waves. High-expenditure flights can be offset by low-advertising hiatus periods. Waves of advertising permit you to gain high visibility when it is needed, followed by reminders during less intense time periods. At the same time, the advertising budget is stretched out so the campaign can cover more of the year.

Share of Advertising

Another type of unanticipated challenge may come from your competitors. If you have more to spend on advertising than any of your competitors do, congratulations! You are in a rare position. Even then, however, you need to turn your dominant share of money into a dominant share of advertising, which is not always as easy as it might seem. It requires at least parity in advertising message strength and competitive efficiency in media selection and buying. Otherwise, the financial advantage will disappear and your firm will be just another part of the competitive pack.

More likely, however, you do not have as much money to spend on advertising as your largest competitor. If your competition is spending at a level that you cannot possibly match, then you will likely choose to advertise in waves. Determining when the waves should run depends on a number of factors: the purchase cycle of your brand, the likelihood of brand-switching by your customers, the anticipated levels of competitive activities, and the life cycle of your brand and your product category.

You can also meet a larger competitor by not trying to match dollar-for-dollar and insertion-for-insertion across the board. Instead, you may be able to match the strongest competitor during parts of the year; if so, why waste money by spreading it thinly throughout the entire year? Another approach is to match your largest competitor in certain markets rather than throughout the entire country. Or you may be more selective in your choice of target audiences; this strategy will give you matching advertising weight against the primary target, even though you may have to sacrifice reaching audiences of lesser importance.

Varying Advertising Scheduling Patterns

There are several reasons why you may wish to vary your advertising placement schedule. Sometimes customers can be unsold by too much advertising. In broadcast, it is possible to induce an "irritation factor," when potential customers become so tired of seeing your advertising that they not only flip channels to avoid seeing your commercial again, but they actually begin to have a negative reaction to the surplus of advertising. Even if you do not advertise so much that you irritate the audience, there is no reason to advertise past the optimum point of exposure; going past the optimum advertising level is wasteful, even when it is not irritating.

If you are using the same advertising schedule from day to day, and you have more than one television commercial that you can run, you may want to alternate the commercials so the viewers do not tire of seeing the same message over and over. If you have only one or two similar commercials, then consider varying the times when they appear so you are not always exposing the same audience to the identical message.

Some products have "life cycles." If your goods fall into this pattern, it may be advisable to reduce or quit advertising for a while, allowing for a "gestation period" when the advertising information can sink in and have an effect.

Sometimes short bursts of advertising, such as in a wave pattern, can produce more sales than a steady amount of heavy advertising. Saving money while gaining greater impact would certainly be attractive, and it would make sense to follow through.

These possibilities may be unique to your brand or to your product category. Because of the differences between products and brands, it is not possible to lay out rules or standards for every kind of advertising media operation. Good research, close observation, and insightful common sense will determine which, if any, of these situations applies to you and how you should proceed.

Starting Date

Many advertising campaigns are scheduled for a year at a time. The year may be a fiscal year or a sales year rather than a calendar year. But no matter what kind of year, the advertising starting date need not necessarily be the first day of the campaign.

Let's say that your advertising is planned for the calendar year. Should you start your advertising placements on January 1? If you have an item that fits appropriately into New Year's parades and football games, maybe you should start then. Most products and services, however, do not fit that mode. New Year's Day advertising is competitive and thus expensive, yet viewers do not always pay close attention; they are often gathered in groups, talking and eating while the television set is on, and some members of the audience are likely to be recovering from the night before. All these factors make New Year's Day a less attractive advertising opportunity—unless, of course, your item fits in well and you can afford it.

Similarly, if your advertising campaign year begins at any other time during the year, you do not necessarily need to begin advertising placements on the very first day. Look at the buying patterns, competitive advertising, your budget, and your preferred waves or other advertising patterns. Base your decisions on your objectives and your strategies, including your scheduling strategies.

Advertising Scheduling

When you plan your campaign schedule, start with a good calendar that includes all the holidays and special events; candy sales increase for Secretaries' Day, an event that is not included on all calendars. Then begin to put together your advertising schedule. Most of the time, the calendar is transferred to a flow chart, which shows the patterns of advertising along with the levels of advertising, all on a sheet or slide that incorporates the proposed advertising schedule, advertising weights, and respective target audiences for the entire campaign period. (See Exhibit 14.2 for an example.)

In addition to your marketing and advertising objectives, your audience targets, your geographic targets, and your scheduling aims, you will want to take into account the creative or message needs and their implications for your advertising media plan. That is the subject of the next chapter.

Political Windows Impact Media Scheduling

By law, political candidates get the lowest media rates offered by a media outlet, along with first rights to that inventory. There are specific times, called political windows, when this law is evoked. Typically, political windows are a six-week period that leads into primary elections (usually in the spring) or a specific election for local, state, or national positions held in November.

The impact of the political window is particularly relevant to advertisers who utilize broadcast media where there are a limited number of commercial units available. The risk that an advertiser runs by scheduling advertising during a political window is that it may not run as scheduled. For example, there have been times in recent history when more than 50 percent of all news commercials have been aired by various political parties. Meanwhile, advertisers that may have booked that time well in advance are left looking for alternative programs or media.

The second impact of the political window is on media costs. Since broadcast properties must sell political commercials at their lowest unit rate, they will be less likely to negotiate low rates with their regular advertisers during these political time periods for fear of losing considerable dollars per unit sold. For these reasons, your role as a savvy advertising media planner becomes even more crucial—and complicated—during an election year.

Chapter 9
Creative Implications

In many advertising agencies, the term "creative department" is used to describe the function whereby the actual advertisements are thought up and illustrated. Sometimes the term "creative" applies only to copywriting; other times, to both copy and layout, which includes art and may involve the art department as well. Even though we are talking about the creative implications for the media portion of the advertising campaign, do not think that creative work can occur only when dealing with copy, layout, and art. There can be creativity involved in media selection and planning, in research, and in other phases of the advertising effort, too; creativity is not limited just to those who write and illustrate the actual advertisements. Perhaps a better term would be "message strategies" or "message functions," as compared to media functions, research functions, production functions, and management functions.

In this discussion, we'll use the terms "creative" and "message" interchangeably, to reflect their use in the advertising industry, while recognizing that there can still be creativity in other advertising functions.

Creative Wants

"We've got to use television. It's the only thing that is able to handle our message," says the copywriting team, while the media team looks at the advertising budget and replies, "Television is completely out of the question. We can't afford it."

Many times, the creative people working on the advertising account will have definite needs that impact the media selection; other times, they have preferences that may not be absolute requirements but that match their initial campaign approaches. For example, if a new shaving cream lends itself well to demonstration, there may be a concomitant need for such media as television, cinema, and the Internet, all of which offer forms of demonstration. Similarly, if vivid color is needed, that requirement may preclude the use of newspapers and of nonvisual media such as radio, while television and the Internet may stay under consideration, and other print media with good color capabilities, such as outdoor billboards and magazines, would be strong candidates for the media campaign.

Other times, however, the creative department may have a preconception about the creative approach that may or may not deserve control over media choices. A copywriter may say, "I envision a television commercial with a woman in a flowing gown, walking through a series of video montages." That may be a nice image, but it is essential to determine whether or not there is a real marketing-, product-, or service-related circumstance that actually requires the use of television or other visual media. It is simply an idea, one that may be accommodated by the media plan if it can be afforded.

In still other instances, the creative department may want to use certain media that are simply not good media choices because they do not reach the target audience. If a creative person indicates that newspapers should be used to distribute coupons for an acne cream, it may be a poor media choice because the likely targets—teenagers—do not tend to read newspapers, either regularly or closely. If you need to reach teens and teens are exposed to radio, cable television, and the Internet, then those are the media that should be considered for the media buys. Don't get locked into preconceptions of how certain media work; for example, coupons and similar offers can be distributed through many kinds of media, not only through print media.

Creative Necessities

As we just saw, there are some instances when there are creative necessities, as opposed to creative wants, that should or even must be accommodated by the media selection process.

Motion and Demonstration

If demonstration is needed to communicate the selling idea, visual media are a must, most likely the Internet, television, and cinema. Similarly, if other kinds of motion are needed, visual media are again indicated.

Do not limit yourself to the most obvious choices, however. The human mind has tremendous capacities for imagination and visualization, even when the visual is not actually present. Tell people to imagine driving a car in the Indianapolis 500, and they may do well providing their own motion pictures in their minds. That approach may not only save media money, but also greatly reduce the cost of production.

Exhibit 9.1

Some Thoughts from an Experienced Media Planner

Maybe the point to be made upfront is that the overall media selection is an *advertising* decision. It requires that media and creative work together on the best approach to get the job done. There may be compromise on either side.

For example, when Motel 6 first broke its Tom Bodett radio campaign on network radio, the media group argued for a :30s because it is half the cost of a :60s. Stan Richards, the principal of the Richards Group, didn't feel that Tom could pull it off in a :30s, so they went to a :60s. It has been one of the most successful campaigns in radio.

On the efficiency side, nearly 50 percent of all network television commercials are :15s, so media planners have had a real impact there.

What we do is a series of trade-off exercises with the creatives to see what is possible. That brings me to the other point, which is the actual creative unit used; that is the other major trade-off on creative. Do we use a magazine full page or can a 2/3 page do the job? How about :30s versus the cost savings and time for the message in :15s on television?

Visuals

If other types of visuals are needed, the media choices can expand to include print media, such as newspapers, magazines, and outdoor advertising. Do not think only of television when visuals are required.

And again, do not limit yourself to even those most obvious choices. Imagine yourself on the first tee at Pebble Beach, or lounging in a hot tub while gazing at the Caribbean and sipping a cool drink. You can see the image in your mind, even though you may never have actually experienced it. In the same way, you can suggest visual images to the audience through radio, sometimes at lower cost and with the resultant higher reach and frequency that the budget will provide.

Coupon Distribution

Mention "coupons" and people automatically think of print media: newspapers and magazines. Outdoor advertising is not considered; how can someone climb up and saw out a coupon portion of the billboard and tote it into the store?

Certainly magazines, newspapers, and direct mail are important media choices for distributing coupons. If you use them, place the coupon near the outer edge of the page so readers can tear out the coupon easily and quickly; most people do not have scissors with them when they are reading, and they do not want to destroy the entire issue just to get at your coupon. But Internet users can print out their own coupons. And coupons can be attached to posters, flyers, or an in-store display.

However, coupons do not have to be actual items provided by the advertisers. Coupons could be almost anything. Ask consumers to get your product and use it as the coupon: "Bring any Pepsi item to the water park this week and get $4 off a regular admission." You may get both sales and the coupon incentive. Even better, get consumers to make their own coupons. When they write out the name of your product, their memories have an even stronger impression of your brand name than when they simply hear or see it. Ask them to print your product name, service logo, or advertising theme on a piece of paper and bring it along in order to save on their purchases. Using couponing in this way, you can utilize almost any advertising medium, including cinema, radio, transit, and outdoor.

Information

When you want to impart specific information to the audience, there may be legitimate media implications. Long passages of detailed wording may not lend themselves to broadcast media but may be handled quite well with some print media and with the Internet.

When providing information in your advertising, your media choices will depend on a number of other factors, such as audience familiarity, message complexity, and legal requirements.

Audience Familiarity

How familiar is the audience with your service or product, or with your advertising theme? They already know what facial tissues do and you do not need to demonstrate them, but they may not understand what a new car-wax wipe does and how it is used, so they may need to see it in action. You need not explain what Dr Pepper is; most already know. But if you have a brand-new soft drink entry, you may need to tell them about it and even show the package.

Message Complexity

A very long or complex message requires adequate space. Sometimes it is possible to read those explanations very rapidly over broadcast media, although nobody will really hear them, or to superimpose passages in small type at the bottom of the screen, although the audience probably will not read them and certainly will not understand them. Billboards do not lend themselves to long passages of body copy, either.

But newspapers and magazines do, as do direct mail and perhaps Internet and in-store displays. Your media choices may be influenced greatly by the complexity and length of the intended message.

Legal Requirements

If you conduct a contest, you must provide certain information about the prizes, odds, entry methods, and purchase requirements and their alternatives. Not all of this information needs to be in the body copy; often, it will be presented in small type as a footnote. Still, it must be there, and including it affects your media choices. You may be able to include such footnotes on a television screen, but they will be read and understood by very few and may only marginally meet the legal standards, and radio may not be conducive at all to including lengthy legal language.

The same considerations apply for including loan requirements, prescription medication caveats, and other similar circumstances.

In-Depth Information

Sometimes you want to include information not because you are required to, but because it enhances your selling message.

For example, you may want to tell consumers how they might make use of a new product; for a new or for an existing product, you may indicate how they might benefit from using it. If you are selling a food product, you may want to induce usage by providing recipes. These message requirements will certainly affect your media choices.

Political Advertising

Selling ideas, whether lobbying for charitable support or running political advertising, may lend itself to certain media. Research shows that audience members are most likely to read and listen to media that tend to agree with their own views: Republicans read Republican newspapers and Democrats read Democratic newspapers, while independents would like to read independent newspapers, if they could find them. To promote a candidate of a certain political party, advertising in media vehicles that are read primarily by the opposition may not be productive, while promoting an independent candidate through those same media vehicles may prove fruitful.

These political considerations take into account the ideas and parties that you are selling, as well as the competing ideas and parties. Considering the competition is vital to successful media selections, as you will see in the next chapter.

Chapter 10

Competitive Analysis

If all we had to do to succeed in advertising media planning was to figure out the right message to send, the right target to receive that message, and the right number of times to send it, advertising planning would be a breeze. However, most brands don't live in isolation. Just as we are trying to persuade the consumer to try our brand, some other brand manager is looking to do the same thing.

Competitive analysis is crucial for establishing a point of difference for your brand as well as for developing the competitive attack plan. Using a competitive analysis in a strategic manner can lead to a number of media strategy decisions. For example, suppose you see a trend emerging where all the competitors in your category are moving their money from television to magazines; that might indicate an opportunity to stand out from the pack by increasing your television exposure. Perhaps your spending is not keeping up with the other brands in the category; this may force you to rethink your national strategy and place greater emphasis on key spot markets where you have the greatest volume.

In today's environment, you must be able to react quickly to competitive threats. Most brands have contingency plans that are based on competitive scenarios. Fortunately, there are a number of competitive information tools on the market today that offer a wealth of data about your brand and the brands against which you compete.

Competitive Tools

There are two major national competitive media tracking tools available for assessing media placement. The larger of the two is Competitive Media Reporting (CMR), which was acquired by TNS Media Intelligence in 2000. The second is Ad*Views, which is owned by Nielsen Media Research. Each service offers a good national overview of media spending. CMR covers a more expansive list of media, while Nielsen's Ad*Views is a bit more in line with the packaged-goods industry.

CMR tracks over 1 million individual brands for 15 media categories. For television, CMR provides actual program-by-program estimated dollars spent and ratings for network and cable. It also offers spending information in the top 100 media markets in the United States, including network and spot radio plus more than 300 Internet Web sites. On the print front, CMR tracks consumer magazines, including Sunday magazines (Sunday supplements), and national and international business print media. CMR also monitors outdoor spending for posters and rotary programs.

Ad*Views tracks media similar to CMR; however, there are some differences. Ad*Views does not cover international print or business-to-business print but does cover free-standing inserts (FSIs), which CMR does not.

The usual lag time between gathering data and actually reporting on it is approximately six weeks. However, both services offer quick topline reports that will allow you to see a competitor's broadcast commercial within a week, so the data can be very current.

Both services are very accurate with their television and consumer print reporting. Local radio is a bit spotty because the services only capture dollars placed through national representatives, while much of local radio spending is done on a local basis. Newspaper inserts are also difficult to measure, and there is no measure of direct mail. However, even with these caveats, the data are relied upon heavily in advertising media planning. Let's take a look at how we can use some of this competitive intelligence.

Share of Spending vs. Share of Voice

The classic way to utilize competitive information is to understand how much your brand spends in relationship to your competitors. Sometimes *share of spending* (SOS) is called *share of voice* (SOV) analysis. Although many media people use these two terms interchangeably, they are different. Share of spending is just that, the percent of total dollars you spent in the category. So share of spending uses absolute dollars as the measuring stick regardless of the medium. In share of spending, a dollar is a dollar whether it is spent on television, print, or outdoor advertising. For example, in 2001, Subway was spending at an $80 million level in the fast food category, which was 6 percent of the total spending. Share of voice, on the other hand, involves the actual impressions delivered as a percent of the total category impressions. Share of voice then takes into account the delivery for each medium, so it draws a distinction between television and print. For example, while Subway represented 6 percent of the total spending, the firm may represent 10 percent of the total impressions in the category because Subway had a more efficient mix of media than the category as a whole. Because these two

Table 10.1

Ratio of SOM to SOS in Quick Service Restaurant Category

Top 10 brands	Share of market (SOM)	Share of spending (SOS)	Ratio
McDonald's	33	30	91
Burger King	14	14	100
Wendy's	10	11	110
Pizza Hut	8	7	88
Taco Bell	8	9	113
Kentucky Fried Chicken (KFC)	7	10	143
Subway	7	8	114
Domino's	5	5	100
Arby's	4	4	100
Dairy Queen	4	2	50
	100	100	100

Source: Brandweek (Technomic Information Services/CMR expenditures).

measures of competitive spending may yield different results, it is extremely important to clarify which analysis is being performed.

SOS or SOV/SOM Analysis

Once you get a grip on your brand's SOS or SOV, you will want to compare those figures to the market-share (*share of market,* or SOM) levels you and your competitors have. This comparison is called either SOS/SOM or SOV/SOM analysis. For example, if your brand has a 30 percent market share with a 15 percent share of category spending, then you would have a ratio of 50; this figure is found by dividing the 30 percent market share into the 15 percent share of spending (15/30). If you are aggressively trying to gain market share, you may want to spend at a level above your current share. If you are the leader in the market, you may want to maintain a spending level equal to your share so that competitors won't erode your market share. Regardless of your strategy, the SOS/SOM analysis is a good building block to guide you to the proper amount you should invest in your brand.

Many studies correlate these two variables. That is why many brand management teams review these calculations. Table 10.1 shows such an example in the fast food category. You will notice that McDonald's, the category leader, has advertising spending that is very much in line with its market share. The other competitors are spending disproportionately in an effort to take market share from McDonald's.

New Brand Introductions

Suppose you had to introduce a new line of frozen entrées into a very crowded category. How much would you spend to introduce them? Without a market share, it is tough to do the SOV/SOM calculation. But competitive spending is still crucial to your budget plans. Most brands estimate the market share that they want to garner in their second year, after the brand is introduced. Then they analyze the competition's spending. New brands typically peg an introductory rate at one-and-a-half to two times that of their Year 2 market share goals. For example, if your goal is to get 5 percent of the frozen entrée market, then you would spend up to 10 percent of the current category spending. This type of analysis is evident in today's marketplace. In 2002, Healthy Choice was spending aggressively at a $17 million level versus market leader Stouffer's at a $10 million level because Healthy Choice was obviously trying to take share from Stouffer's.

Media Strategy

Competitive spending is a good strategic tool for making media decisions. The Heath candy bar was a small brand that faced strong competition in the category. The majority of spending was done leading into Halloween. While Heath's sales spiked in October, it had another spike around Easter, when category spending was less pronounced. Heath shifted its spending to emphasize Easter and other key times of the year when the brand could make an impact.

Another strategy decision might be in the media choice itself. If the majority of the category dollars are going to television and you have the opportunity to stand out in radio, then shifting your advertising to radio might be worth considering.

Competitive spending can also be used to determine tactical decisions: In what specific daypart could your brand make an impact? Is there a creative unit that you might want to use to tell your story? Is there a specific day or days of the week when it may be more beneficial for your brand to run its spot?

All of these questions point to competitive gaps that can be exploited. So, when approaching media strategy, ask yourself if there is something that you can do to stand out from your competitors.

This is certainly the case in the frozen dinner and entrée category shown in Table 10.2. Because Healthy Choice and Stouffer's dominate the spending, other brands are forced to look at alternative media in order to stand out. Weight Watcher Smart Ones puts all its money in magazines to make

Table 10.2

Media Mix Comparison: Frozen Dinners and Entrées

Brand	Total media (millions)	Percent allocation		
		Network TV	Spot TV	Magazines
Stouffer's	10.3	50	5	45
Lean Cuisine Lite Classics	5.7	—	50	50
Smart Ones	2.7	—	—	100
Healthy Choice	17.2	60	20	20
Source: Brandweek (CMR expenditures).				

an impact in a certain medium, while Lean Cuisine Lite Classics allocates a significant amount of its resources to spot television in order to be competitive in selective market areas.

Advertising-to-Sales Ratios

Another use of competitive spending analysis is to determine the advertising-to-sales ratios for your competitors to see what percent of their revenue they are spending on media advertising. Advertising-to-sales ratio is calculated by dividing the total advertising expenditures by the total amount of brand sales or revenue. For example, Healthy Choice was a $230 million brand spending $17.2 million on advertising. Healthy Choice's advertising-to-sales ratio was 7.5 percent. Contrast those figures to Stouffer's, a $475 million brand spending at a $10 million level or an advertising-to-sales ratio of 2.1 percent. Healthy Choice was spending almost twice the amount of Stouffer's on an absolute basis and more than three times that amount on a percent of sales basis (See Table 10.3).

Determining Trends in Spending

Another great use of competitive spending information is to calculate trend-line analysis. The media planner should be updating such an analysis every year. You want to see whether spending in the category is increasing or decreasing over time and at what rate. You can compare this result to the sales growth in the category to determine the vitality of the category. If the category is growing at only 2 percent per year in sales, yet advertising is growing at a 10 percent rate, it tells you that a healthy return is going to be tougher to attain. Conversely, if you have a fast-growing category with

Table 10.3

Advertising-to-Sales Ratio

	Healthy Choice	Stouffer's
Sales	$230.0 million	$475.0 million
Advertising expenditures	$17.2 million	$10.0 million
Advertising-to-sales ratio	7.5 percent	2.1 percent

Source: Brandweek (CMR expenditures).

slower advertising growth, it might suggest that you could step up your own support of the brand.

Trends can be helpful to identify a change in spending patterns over time. Perhaps the category is gradually moving money from television into print, or maybe dollars once funneled into the fourth quarter are now in the third quarter. Over time, you can see how the category is behaving and use this information to help chart your media course.

Marketing-Mix Models

Many brands today are conducting sophisticated marketing-mix modeling. This research is made possible by the availability of a tremendous amount of consumer data. With so many grocery chains using loyalty programs that capture individual purchase behavior, the ability to track purchases and relate them to various marketing elements is a ready-made laboratory. Both Nielsen and IRI utilize these purchase data and work with manufacturers on developing marketing-mix models. They combine this robust information with powerful multivariate statistical analysis to determine what aspects of the marketing mix are most effective. One element of designing a marketing-mix model is the brand's media spending and the competitors' spending. Marketing-mix models can help brand managers understand the impact of all their marketing elements, as well as how individual media perform.

For example, in Table 10.4 we see that our fictitious brand, Bob's Beans, is extremely sensitive to advertising. For every dollar that Bob's Beans spends on media advertising, the brand receives a return of $1.50. This return is much higher than the return from using an FSI with a coupon or using trade promotions. So, based on this analysis, Bob's Beans should be an aggressive advertiser.

Each brand is going to have its own set of dynamics: one may be especially advertising sensitive, while another may respond well only to trade

Table 10.4

Marketing Mix Model: Bob's Beans

Item	Incremental profit per $1 spent
Media advertising	$1.50
FSI coupons	$1.00
Trade promotions	$0.85

promotion or couponing. With the power of these customer databases, much of what works and what doesn't work can be explained. Competitive media spending plays a crucial role in this sophisticated analysis.

Competitive spending information is a powerful tool for media planning. It can lead to breakout strategies, help determine specific spending levels, and be trended and analyzed within sophisticated marketing models. Competitive spending can be significant in setting communication goals, which we will discuss in the next chapter.

Online Competitive Analysis

As more and more advertisers utilize interactive marketing strategies, keeping up to date on your competitor's online strategy is crucial to most brands. While certain online spending is similar to other media, the aspect of *search engine marketing* (SEM) is not.

All other competitive media spending reports contain the media schedules and the estimated media costs of that schedule for a given competitor. However, because SEM is done on a bid basis, it is impossible for a service to truly estimate the amount of dollars allocated to SEM by a competitor. Table 10.5 shows an example of both SEM and banner advertising for the athletic shoe category. SEM competitive spending is reported in the number of SEM impressions. There is no estimated spending for those impressions. However, you can get a deep understanding of the SEM strategy since these competitive reports also include the specific keywords that a competitor has included in their SEM campaign.

For banner advertising, there is an estimated media spending amount provided for these impressions. Banner advertising in this case can mean anything from static banners to rich media. The specific creative unit is detailed in the media planning report so you can understand the mix of creative elements being deployed in a competitor's online campaign, as well as the specific sites where they advertises.

Table 10.5

Nielsen/NetRatings Ad Relevance
Impressions and Estimated Spending by Category for Custom Advertiser
"Athletic Shoes"

Company	SEM Impressions (000)	Banner Impressions (000)	Estimated Banner Spending
Nike, Inc.	17,282	789,315	$4,704,400
Adidas-Salomon Ltd.	13,485	425,898	$2,164,700
Reebok International Ltd.	7,356	177,366	$731,500
Skechers USA, Inc.	11,185	101,642	$329,500
New Balance Athletic Shoe, Inc.	12,128	471,930	$262,700
ASICS Corporation		4	$0
Total	61,436	1,966,155	$8,192,800

Source: NetRatings, Inc.

Chapter 11

Setting Media Communications Goals

Once you have determined whom you want to reach, where they are, and when you need to reach them, you must determine how much pressure you need to put behind your message. This is where media communications goals come into play. Setting communications goals can be a difficult challenge. It is like someone with a weakness for sweets going into an ice cream shop: you want it all, but you have to make some tough choices.

Communications goals are often reduced to the big four dimensions. The first dimension is *reach:* which potential customers do you want to reach? The second dimension is *frequency:* how often do you want to reach them? The third dimension is *continuity:* how many days, weeks, months, and patterns of advertising do you need at the appropriate reach and frequency levels? Another consideration is *impact:* how large do you want print advertisements to be, and how long do you want broadcast commercials to run?

The first data point you need to consider is your brand's purchase cycle.

Product Purchase Cycle

The brand's product purchase cycle is going to be the lead factor in determining how many weeks you need to advertise. Suppose you market a brand of Christmas candy, and 90 percent of your sales are done in the four or five weeks between Thanksgiving and Christmas. You would likely set your communications goals on a weekly basis for that critical period or prior to it to account for the lag effect of advertising.

Conversely, suppose that you are marketing a brand of bread. Consumers buy bread every week of the year. You may set a weekly purchase cycle, but then you need to cover a lot of weeks.

Most packaged-goods brands have product purchase cycles of three to four weeks. That means that the consumer is buying the brand about once a month. As a result, many media planners use four weeks as the benchmark for developing reach and frequency estimates. Most reach and frequency models are built on this four-week curve also because one week's advertising may have an unusual pattern, while four weeks' worth shows a more typical pattern.

It is important to know your brand's purchase cycle. It forms the frame of reference for establishing reach and frequency goals, as well as continuity.

Setting Reach Goals

Now that you know your brand's purchase cycle, you are ready to establish reach and frequency goals. Suppose that you are marketing an established frozen-dinner line. The brand's product purchase cycle is four weeks. You want to set your reach and frequency levels to that four-week period.

First, let's tackle the reach dimension. To continue to grow the brand, you want to reach the majority of your consumers with some sort of message within that four-week time frame. Let's set a goal of 80 percent target reach.

How did you get to 80 percent? Media planners can run an analysis of how much it costs to reach your audience. There is a point at which it is difficult to get incremental reach. Typically, that point begins around 80 percent. So that is why you don't set your goal at 90 percent.

Why not less than 80 percent? Assuming that the brand needs to reach the majority of its consumers, you pick the point at which it is most economical to do just that. Reaching less than 80 percent seems like you would be leaving revenue on the table.

This doesn't mean that you should always set 80 percent as the reach level. There are reasons to set it lower and reasons to set it higher. Most brands rarely set their reach goals at less than 50 percent for the purchase cycle; rather, they stay in the two-thirds to four-fifths range.

Setting Frequency Goals

Now that you have the reach level established, how many times should you reach your potential customers? In the above example, you set your goals based on a four-week purchase cycle. It seems like common sense that you would want to reach your consumer at least one time per week, an average of four times per month.

Most reach and frequency goals use the average-frequency concept. Whether it is three, four, five, or even 20, that is the average number of times a consumer would see or hear your brand's commercial message in a given time frame.

Table 11.1

**Frequency Distribution for 80 Percent Reach, 4.0 Average
Frequency Television Schedule**

Frequency	Exposed (%)	Exposed at least (%)
1	17.4	80
2	11.9	63
3	8.5	51
4	6.3	42
5	4.7	36
6	3.6	31
7	2.8	28
8	2.2	25
9	1.7	23
10+	5.2	21

Note: Based on women 25 to 54 years old, multiple dayparts.
Source: Telmar.

In this example, we have a reach goal of 80 percent and an average frequency goal of 4.0 within the four-week time frame. However, 80 percent of the consumers aren't exposed to your message four times each. Some may see it only once, while others may see it eight times or more. Because it is an average, half will likely see it fewer than four times while half will see it more than four times.

This dynamic of frequency of exposure has led media planners to set certain levels of effective frequency.

Effective Frequency

Research studies indicate that consumers do not retain an advertising message until they have seen it at least three times. This figure is the basis for effective frequency—that point at which the advertising frequency becomes effective or motivating. Many media planners use 3.0+ as the sacred rule of thumb because this body of research is so compelling.

Media planners then translate effective frequency into effective reach level—the percentage of the audience reached more than three times. In the case of the 80 percent reach at an average frequency of 4.0, the effective reach or percent of consumers exposed 3.0+ times is 51 percent, which means that half of the consumers have been effectively reached (See Table 11.1).

Setting an effective frequency goal and subsequent reach level can be a good way to establish a delivery goal. In this example, you want to reach at least 50 percent of your audience 3.0+ times within a given four-week purchase cycle.

We have used 3.0+ as the effective frequency level. However, the majority of that research was done in the 1970s with mature brands. So is 3.0+ always the standard for effectiveness? No. Is there value in the first or second impression that a consumer sees? Yes.

Developing the appropriate effective frequency level is as much an art as a science. There are factors that might suggest more frequency or less frequency. Weights can be applied to the first and second impressions ranging from 100 percent effective to 25 percent effective, depending upon message strength and creative approach.

Setting the effective frequency level can be a complex process. Let's look at some of the factors that might affect your decision.

Communications Matrix

Obviously, you want to reach your target audience at least once. So the real question becomes, how many more times do you need to reach them with your message before it sinks in and motivates them to act? While this is the $64,000 question, there are some commonsense ways to narrow it down.

For example, if you were introducing a new brand, you would need to have more frequency than you'd need for an established brand. The same would be true if your brand had very low awareness.

Perhaps you are in a category that has had a number of new entries, and the marketplace is becoming a real dogfight. That may warrant more frequency to just maintain your current position in the category.

The advertising message can also have an impact on the amount of frequency you assign—say, if you have new copy that would warrant more frequency to seed the message. Or if you had a limited-time offer that expires in a week, then you would want more frequency to ensure that it is noticed and remembered.

Table 11.2 shows a frequency-planning matrix that takes into account brand maturity, awareness, competition, the newness of the copy, and the type of message that is to be advertised.

Depending upon where your brand falls in relation to these elements, you simply add the outcome to the base level of one. If your brand is more than five years old, totally dominates the category, has over 90 percent awareness with every audience available, faces no competition, and has a brand campaign that is over two years old, then we applaud you. Based on this matrix, you don't need to advertise. We have yet to meet that brand manager, so until we do, the matrix stands as an example of how to assign values to get the appropriate frequency level or effective frequency.

Table 11.2

Frequency Planning Matrix

| Factor | Add to base level of 1 | | |
	High (1)	Average (0)	Low (−1)
Brand maturity	New	Brand in market 2–5 years	Brand in market 5+ years
Brand awareness	New or low awareness	Average awareness	Strongly established leader
Competitive category	Very aggressive	Some spending but your brand is on par	Little spending. Your brand has over 50 percent share
Advertising campaign	New campaign/ message	In second year	Has run for 2+ years
Type of response	Short-term promotion	Mix of promo/ brand	Long-term brand

Just to put the matrix to the test, let's suppose that you were introducing a new product into a heavily advertised category. Because your brand is new and has no awareness, you would add frequency to the base of one. Also, you have a new campaign and a very competitive category, so you add frequency there as well. While you are using short-term promotional tactics such as coupons and price promotions in-store to gain immediate trial, you have decided that your advertising message will be a brand-differentiation message that is in for the long haul. Using the matrix, you come to the effective frequency level of four, so you would peg your objectives to reaching so many of your target consumers four or more times within a given product purchase cycle.

So those are ways of defining effective frequency solutions to your brand's communications problems. Effective frequency is certainly a viable method for developing communications goals. But it is not the only one. In the past few years, we have seen the rise of a new philosophy called *recency* (See Table 11.3).

Recency

Recency theory suggests that you want to have your advertising impressions as close to the point of sale as possible. So recency theory puts much more emphasis on being constantly in the market with advertising rather than being in the market only with a higher level of impact or effective frequency. Recency planning has been in vogue in the past years particularly with

Table 11.3

Recency Planning Matrix, New Product Introduction in Heavily Advertised Category

	Add to base level of 1			
Factor	High (1)	Average (0)	Low (−1)	Comment
Brand awareness	X			New product with no awareness
Competitive category	X			Highly competitive category
Advertising campaign	X			New ad campaign
Type of response			X	Long-term brand
Brand maturity	X			New introductions
	4	0	−1	= 3 incremental + 1 base level = 4+ frequency level

mature brands that need to remind consumers constantly to purchase them. It has proven to be a very effective strategy in that regard.

In recency planning, the emphasis is on covering as many product purchase cycles as possible. Many recency plans use weekly goals of, say, a 60 percent reach with a one frequency but advertise on the air 75 percent or more of the weeks of the year.

While the term *recency* is a relatively new one, the concept of continuous advertising is not. As Vernon Baird, the head of Mrs. Baird's Bakeries until his death in 1992, was heard to say, "Advertising is as important an ingredient as flour. People buy my bread every day and I advertise every day." His strategy seems to have paid off: Baird's became the number one brand of bread in Texas while store brands dominated almost every other state.

Continuity vs. Impact

We have now discussed *effective frequency,* which determines the desired frequency level at which you want to advertise, and *recency,* which is a lower-level, continuity approach to advertising. So which approach is the best?

Each approach has its own merits. There is no one size that fits all. As we have discussed, it all depends on your brand's situation and relationship to the category in which it competes.

If you have a new brand or are restaging an old brand, then you are more likely to use the effective frequency concept for setting your communications goals. If you are in charge of a mature brand that is consistently purchased and you need that constant contact with a broad target group, then you are more likely to go down the recency path.

As with most strategies, there are hybrid strategies that come from either side. The real trade-off becomes the amount of media weight in a given purchase cycle versus the number of purchase cycles with media weight.

Let's say that your brand is canned green beans and that you can afford 1,800 target rating points (TRP) a year. Let's assume that canned green beans have a relatively flat seasonal purchase skew and are purchased every four weeks.

For the same budget dollars, you could schedule 60 TRP for 30 weeks and cover nearly 60 percent of the year with your advertising, or you could schedule 120 TRP a week and cover 15 weeks of the year. One schedule offers continuity and the other impact. It is the age-old trade-off.

In this case, being on the air more weeks than not seems like the best course of action, particularly if each week basically represents approximately 2 percent of sales. The one schedule covers around 60 percent of sales, while the other covers only 30 percent of sales. So the impact of the second schedule must be worth two times that of the first schedule for it to pay out.

Response Goals for Communications

Throughout this chapter, we have discussed setting communications goals based largely on achieving brand awareness. This is a typical approach to media planning, regardless of the type of industry or brand that is being advertised. However, reach, frequency, and continuity of exposure are all just different means to the same end. That end can range from an awareness gain to a change in attitude to generating more traffic to a store. Regardless of your situation, you are looking for some form of response from your advertising dollars.

Another way to approach setting communications goals is to start with the response that you are trying to achieve and working backward. For example, if you have an advertising budget of $1,000 and you know that you need to generate $10,000 in incremental sales to be successful, you now have a goal. If you also know that the average customer spends $50 in your store, then your advertising must generate 200 additional customers for you to be successful. Armed with these facts, you now know that you have a ceiling of $5 per new customer, or your advertising will not pay out. (This rate was calculated by dividing the $1,000 ad budget by 200 new customers.)

So, if your media plan has a mix of media that costs 10 cents per person, it would generate 10,000 impressions. If 2 percent of these people respond to your offer, you are home free.

The point of this exercise is that sales response is a crucial component to setting communications goals. Whether it is through sophisticated marketing mix models or just looking at next-day sales, the response to advertising is the barometer for how much advertising you are likely to do. This type of information is vital to media planners as they begin to construct a plan. There is no sense in coming in with a plan that won't deliver the expected results. Over time, most brands have a track record of what works and what doesn't. Using response information in conjunction with reach and frequency analysis is an excellent method of determining how many resources you should allocate toward a campaign.

Response analysis is the core of setting communications goals for online media. Since online media have built-in response analysis tools, online plans are highly measurable. Most online campaigns have specific response goals established as benchmarks prior to the campaign. As the campaign unfolds, the online media professional begins to adjust creative or media strategies to meet these goals.

Conclusion

Setting communications goals is a complex task. However, much of it involves commonsense decisions. The first step in the process is to understand your brand's purchase dynamics. From there you can assess the appropriate levels of reach and frequency necessary to achieve the specific advertising response. It is important to meld reach and frequency information with any sales or other response metrics to build the appropriate communications goals.

Chapter 12

How to Prepare an Advertising Media Plan

When you propose an advertising media plan, you need to keep several things in mind: logic throughout the plan, sensible progression from one stage of the plan to another, fully explaining and justifying every recommended decision, and meeting the stated objectives.

The steps in a media plan are fairly straightforward. Most plans use a format similar to the one illustrated in Exhibit 12.1.

Overview or Executive Summary

As with most business reports and proposals, we start with an overview, often called an executive summary, in which major recommendations are summarized. This summary should not be used to tell you, the advertiser, things you already know about yourself, your company, and your brand. Instead, this section should be a summary of the media recommendations that are contained in the body of the report.

Use the executive summary to preview what is to come. With this advance knowledge, you can read and make more sense of the actual proposed media plan. Some top executives may read only this summary, but the brand manager needs to read and study the entire proposal, using the overview to provide background information and expectations before getting into the heart of the media plan.

Ironically, even though the executive summary is the first section of the media plan, it cannot be written until the rest of the plan is completed because it provides a review of the entire proposal.

Competitive Analysis

Complete analysis of your major competitors should be detailed in your media plan, along with the competitors' marketing and advertising efforts

Exhibit 12.1

Outline of a Media Plan

An advertising media plan may take more than one approach and there is no industry-wide outline that is always used. The organization below includes the necessary topics and can serve as a guide to prepare a media proposal for an advertising campaign.

Overview/executive summary
Competitive analysis
Market situation
Objectives and goals
    Marketing objectives
    Advertising objectives
    Media objectives
Media strategies
    Targets
        Markets
        Groups
        Audiences
    Media types
Media tactics
    Media vehicles
    Media units
    Media schedule
Media promotions
Media logistics
Continuity plans
Calendar
Budget
Integrated marketing and media

and their targets and media used. It is essential that the competition be analyzed thoroughly and completely before getting into the objectives. Because some of the objectives will likely deal with meeting the competition, the competitive analysis is an important input to those objectives.

Market Situation

If the marketplace is complex and its analysis cannot be covered in the competitive analysis, it will require a separate section. Again, information needs to be analyzed prior to the formation of objectives.

Objectives and Goals

Next come the actual objectives, what you will try to accomplish with your advertising media plan. There are usually three categories of objectives: overall marketing objectives, advertising objectives, and media objectives.

Marketing Objectives

The marketing objectives deal with the overall selling goals. They may be established at the corporate or company level, or at the marketing level. The advertising staff may be involved in establishing the marketing objectives, but oftentimes the objectives have already been set by the time the advertising media planner gets them, leaving little chance for input or adjustment to these goals.

Advertising Objectives

Similarly, the advertising objectives are essential. They must support the overall marketing objectives and focus on the overall advertising effort, including the research, message, visual, and media phases of the advertising campaign. Again, the media planner may be given these advertising objectives and told to follow them; fortunate is the media planner who has a chance to provide input and to influence the advertising objectives.

As is the case for all objectives, the advertising objectives need to be spelled out in detail, with thorough justification of each one.

Media Objectives

The media objectives must be consistent with the overall advertising objectives, which in turn must complement the overriding marketing objectives. In fact, sometimes the marketing objectives and advertising objectives are summarized here, providing lead-ins to and references for the media objectives. Look back at chapter 5 for examples of the various topics that might be included under each type of objective.

Media Strategies

Remember that strategies are plans, so this section contains the actual plans that are proposed to meet the media objectives.

Targets

Although some media planners include the targets in their objectives, in many ways, the targets are part of the planning to meet the objectives, rather than objectives in themselves. Therefore, it often makes more sense to place the targets in the strategic phase of the plan.

Targets should be fully described and their selection should be justified. There are at least three types of targets that may be considered.

Target Markets

If the term *markets* is limited to geographic areas, then the geographic planning for the media campaign will be spelled out here.

Target Groups

The kinds of people that the media plan will attempt to reach, usually outlined in demographic terms, are given here.

Target Audiences

Because there is no advertising medium that reaches all of a target market or target group and only that target market or group, the media audiences will often be defined separately.

Media Types

Remember that advertising media are ways of achieving ends: they are not objectives in and of themselves. That is why the media to be used are included as strategies rather than goals. The selection of each advertising medium proposed for a campaign must be fully justified. In addition, other advertising media that were considered and not selected should also be listed, along with the reasons for not using them.

Media Tactics

The tactics are the implementation of the plan—the actual advertising campaign being carried out. Even though the tactics do not come into play until the proposed media plan is approved, there still should be some discussion at this point of the tactics to be used and complete justification of each.

Media Vehicles

It is likely that the media types will be spelled out in the strategies section, but the individual media vehicles to be used might not be. Under *tactics,* each specific media vehicle selection should be discussed and then justified.

Media Units

The length of broadcast commercials, size of print advertisements, and specifications such as the use of bleed, color, and the like should be presented here, again with justification.

Media Schedule

The advertising campaign schedule may be discussed in the advertising objectives, or it may be set earlier. Still, there should be some detail on the proposed timing of the advertising, including starting and stopping dates, flight and hiatus plans, levels of advertising, coordination of scheduling across the various media, and recognition of the selling calendar and other timing factors. Again, justification is required.

Media Promotions

If the use of nonadvertising promotions is not discussed anywhere else, it should be included here. Although its proposed use may come in an earlier section, it is most likely to appear in the tactical stage.

Media Logistics

Support activities such as special media research, photography, print and broadcast production, and similar concerns may need to be treated, discussed, and justified.

Contingency Plans

The contingency plans should be complete enough to be used if they are actually needed. If something in the original campaign must be changed, it will likely be on short notice, leaving little opportunity to develop complete plans in a high-pressure situation.

See the detailed discussion of contingency plans back in chapter 5.

Calendar

The scheduling may be discussed elsewhere in your media plan, but it is a good idea to have one central place where the media and promotion schedules can be included. This schedule is often presented in the form of a flow chart.

See chapter 14 for an example of a flow chart or brand-planning calendar.

Budget

The advertising media budget needs to be presented, with allocations shown for each major type of medium and other major uses, along with any necessary explanation and complete rationale.

Integrated Marketing

Because so many firms make use of integrated marketing, the integration of the advertising media plan into the overall marketing picture may need to be disclosed. The use of integrated marketing communications and of integrated media, if used, can also be included here.

Conclusion

You can see, then, that a media plan needs justification and rationale at every stage, along with a logical progression from objectives through strategies to tactics and outcomes. Check back to make sure that all the media objectives are being dealt with and can be accomplished.

A solid media plan is vital to bringing a successful conclusion to your advertising and marketing efforts.

Chapter 13

Evaluating an Advertising Media Plan

As with so many professional tasks, evaluating a proposed advertising media plan requires experience and knowledge. Such evaluations are much easier after you have seen a few others, and even better once you have been exposed to dozens of them.

Even if you do not have a high degree of experience, there are still some major and minor factors to watch for, examine carefully, and use to determine whether the media plan seems to be "on track" or is just a random collection of haphazard ideas.

Format

The format of a good media plan should be clear, logical, and easy to read and follow. The format should take you through the entire process, from the background information on which the plan was based to the current situation and on through the hoped-for goals and objectives. Then it should move from objectives into strategies and plans, the methods that will be used to achieve the goals and objectives, including the types of media to be used. Next are the tactics to implement the plans, which might include media vehicles and units. There may also be a final section that involves the necessary support activities, such as research, production, and checking.

Any media plan will be judged more favorably if it looks good; as in real estate or in meeting new people, first impressions are important, and a sloppy plan that is not carefully crafted and assembled will likely receive a poor evaluation.

Is there a table of contents, with page numbers, included in the plan? Does that table of contents make logical sense, and does it match up with the actual pages on which the corresponding materials appear?

Are the pages numbered and assembled in proper order? An upside-down or backwards page creates the impression of poor planning and hurried thinking.

Starting each new section of the plan on a new page, using double-spacing, including graphics and tables, and providing full explanations will also create a better impression in the evaluation.

Overview

The overview or executive summary should be the first element in the media plan, even though it cannot be written until all the other sections have been completed. The overview lets the reader see what is coming, so that he or she is not forced to read through it all twice. For the senior executive, the overview gives the essential information and answers the questions: Who are the targets, where are they located, and what media will be used to reach them?

It is important not to give too much information in the overview. For example, including the history of the client firm is unnecessary; after all, the client will know this history better than the media planner ever could.

Current Situation and Competition

There should be some treatment of the current marketing situation—the problem that this media plan is attempting to overcome.

In addition, there must be detailed information about the competition. It is not possible to establish the advertising and media objective without first considering the competition. This section should include not just general competitive information but also detailed insights into the competitors' uses of advertising and media. And all competitors should be included, not just the major ones.

Objectives

It is essential that objectives are set early and followed throughout the rest of the media plan. The objectives and goals must be explained, with complete rationale and justification.

Too often, strategies, such as the types of media to be used, are included in the objectives. It is important that this section include only what is to be accomplished—the goals—and that the strategies to achieve them be held back. Media, after all, are strategies, not objectives. Using television or magazines is not a goal; the goal is to sell, to convince, to change opinions, to inform, and to communicate, and the media are strategies that will be used in the plans to achieve these ends.

Media planning objectives should be specific rather than vague. The best objectives will be quantified with actual goal numbers stated, so it is clear at the end of the campaign whether the objectives have been reached.

Targets

There should be three kinds of targets: *target markets,* which are the geographic areas and cities where advertising will be focused; *target groups,* which are the kinds of people the advertising will reach, usually given in demographic terms; and *target audiences,* which are the people that can actually be reached through advertising in the mass media.

For example, the advertising for the Hyundai Accent automobile may be aimed at lower-income persons in some large metropolitan areas, but there is no advertising medium that reaches those persons, only those persons, and all of those persons; therefore, the target audience may be slightly different from the target group and target market.

Targets are sometimes given as part of the objectives, although it may make more sense for the targets to be included with strategies and plans, because they are a means of accomplishing the goals and objectives.

Targets are typically described in prose in a media plan, but they should also include a numerical component. How many people (in thousands and as a percentage) are you aiming for, and how often will they be reached? Do these numbers make sense, and do they match up with the numerical targets?

Like every other section of the media plan, the targets should be fully explained and justified. They are important and deserve complete attention and treatment. Why these targets and not others? How were these decisions made and why?

In addition, the media planner must determine whether the targets are feasible. If the goal is to cover all 50 United States, and the target is for only the top 10 or 15 markets in the country, that target may be too small a portion of the country to do an effective job. In addition, reaching only a small portion the markets would make it difficult if not impossible to achieve sales-level goals.

Strategies

Strategies are plans—the plans that will be used to achieve the campaign objectives. As mentioned above, these strategies may include the targets. And the strategies will certainly include the media that are being recommended for inclusion in the campaign.

These media cannot possibly be selected before the objectives and the targets have been detailed. After all, a medium is by definition a go-between, so it must be clear what the goal is before any medium or go-between can be determined. Similarly, the target must be clearly defined before media can be selected, because it is not possible to know which media will reach those targets until the targets are clear.

The reasons for using each medium must be spelled out in detail. In addition, and just as important, is one fact that is too often overlooked: the reasons for not using other media. It should be clear that all possible media were considered and judged fairly in their applicability to the situation, to the campaign objectives, and to the targets to be reached.

It is not enough simply to give media types, however. For the media being recommended, what specific newspaper and magazines, which broadcast programs and stations, which cable networks are being suggested? And, as always, there must be compelling reasons to justify every decision, strategy, and tactic.

Budget

Now comes the money, an essential element in any campaign. Is there enough money to do an adequate job? Are the monies being spread too thinly across too many targets or too many media? Is there enough money to do an adequate job in each medium and against each target group?

It only makes sense to allocate money to each medium. In the case of local-market media, such as spot radio and local newspapers, the total sum for that medium must be reallocated to individual cities and markets. It makes no sense to allocate all the monies to individual markets if some of the media choices are national in scope, because then those individual-market allocations would have to be re-added together for the national buys.

Allocations to media and markets should be explained and justified. The budget should be given in a coordinated budgetary overview, and the allocation of funds to various types of media should be determined prior to the tactical phase of the plan.

Contingency Plan

Toward the end of the media plan, there should be a contingency plan, with details on what will be done if the proposed plan is not working as anticipated. Contingency plans are often too brief and oversimplified to be of any real use. In an emergency, there is no time to come up with alternative plans, so the contingency plan is vital.

Again, justification is needed.

Schedule

There also needs to be a schedule or calendar showing what advertising will be running during each phase of the campaign. This schedule is often given in the form of a flow chart because it can combine the media to be used, the weights for each medium, the time span, and the overlapping uses of various media. A presentation of the calendar in a flow chart or some other visually appealing graphic makes this information easier to communicate and easier to understand. (See Exhibits 13.1–13.5 for media checklists.)

Overall

General standards to consider include: (1) When information or data are provided, the sources of those facts should also be provided so the reader can judge the quality and reliability of the information. Keep in mind, too, that information gained from the Internet is often spurious or questionable. (2) When tables or figures or similar data are included, they should be related to the plans and objectives rather than simply dropped in with little apparent connection to the overall media plan. (3) When various terms are used, they should be clearly defined. Not everybody agrees on the meaning of every specialized term or expression. (4) The plan should not be too general or oversimplified. The more information and detail included, the better. (4) If a media plan starts strongly and then becomes much more general or just falls apart at the end, it is usually an indication that the planner started too late and ran out of time to complete the job. (5) Writing is important, too, so the written plan should utilize good grammar and correct spelling, with no typographical or punctuation errors. It may also be a good idea to avoid slang and abbreviations in formal business reports. Write from the advertiser's perspective, not your own; after all, this is the advertiser's plan and money. (6) Finally, as stressed earlier, justification is key to a successful media plan. An advertising budget may involve large sums of money, and the proposed expenditure of those funds needs to be sound.

Exhibit 13.1

Media Checklist

I.   Marketing goals
   A. Is the plan designed to:
      1. increase usage from existing user base?
      2. increase usage from lighter users?
      3. increase trial among nonusers?
      4. protect current user base from erosion?
II. Advertising goals
   A. Is the plan designed to:
      1. increase awareness among the target?
      2. change perception of the target(s)?
      3. generate an immediate response?
      4. generate an inquiry?
III. Timing
   A. Do you know the fiscal year?
   B. Is there a specific start date?
   C. What is the plan period?
IV. Target audience
   A. For consumer goods, have you defined the target(s)?
      1. usage (heavy, medium, light)
      2. demographics
      3. PRIZM clusters
      4. need-based segments
      5. drawn-out specific target segments with names
      6. looked at MRI, media audit
      7. looked at Spectra for packaged goods
      8. purchaser vs. user
      9. purchaser influencer
   B. For B2B clients, have you defined target(s)?
      1. standard industrialization classification code
      2. job description
      3. demographics
      4. need-based segments
      5. influencers in decision chain

V.   Seasonality
   A. Have you looked at the following:
      1. sales by month or week?
      2. category sales vs. brand sales?
      3. competitive activity vs. sales?
VI. Geography
   A. Is the plan national, international, or local?
      1. Do you have sales by markets?
      2. Do you have category sales by market?
      3. Have you calculated BDI/CDI?
         a. Do you know distribution by market?
         b. ACV for packaged goods?
         c. Number of stores/units for retailers?
VII. Creative considerations
   A. Are creative units determined for media?
      1. If so, what are they?
      2. If not, what should they be?
      3. Are units in sync with goal and budget?
VIII. Budget
   A.   Do you know the total budget?
   B.   What is the media budget?
   C.   Is it net or gross?
   D.   How does it compare to last year?
   E.   How does it compare to competition?
   F.   Have you calculated share of market (SOM) to share of spending (SOS)?
   G.   What is the ad-to-sales ratio?
IX. Mandatories
   A. Are there any sacred cows?
   B. Has the client purchased anything on his own?
X.   Communications goals
   A. Have you set up specific communications goals?
      1. Reach/Frequency
         a. Is there an effective frequency level?
      2. Have you used the matrix?
      3. Is there a continuity goal?
      4. Is continuity more important than higher weight levels?

(continued)

Exhibit 13.1 *(continued)*

XI. Media strategies
  A. Do your media strategies include:
    1. Which media mix is best?
    2. How to best use each medium?
XII. Media tactics
  A. Do your tactics include:
    1. What is best vehicle and why?
    2. Cost analysis?
    3. Target audience analysis?
  B. Can you own a vehicle?
  C. Include a flowchart?
  D. Include a budget recap?
  E. Compare this year to last year?
  F. Have alternative plans?
XIII. Test options
  A. Is there the option of testing?
    1. Higher spend level?
    2. Alternative media mix?
    3. Different target?
    4. Different buying strategy?

Source: FKM.

Exhibit 13.2

Media Checklist: Retail

Retail advertising can be slightly more complicated than other advertising, and it is often different even when it is not more complicated. Here is a checklist for retail advertising media plans; use this checklist in addition to the checklist used for all advertising media plans.

1. Do you know what comp store sales goal is?
2. Do you have daily sales and know when key holidays are?
   • How have holidays changed vs. one year ago?
3. Do you know where the stores are located?
   • Have you defined a trading radius (e.g., 3 miles)?
4. Is the target audience different by trading area or market?
   • Are there pockets of consumer opportunity?
5. Do you know how print is planned?
   • What dates are they planned to run?
6. How was media planned year to year?
   • Many retailers comp on a weekly basis.
7. Competition is crucial for retail. Do you have a handle on when and where the competition spend?

Source: FKM.

Exhibit 13.3

Media Checklist: Packaged Goods

1. Do you know the source of volume for marketing mix?
    - Has a marketing-mix study been done?
2. Do you have volume and incremental volume goals?
3. Do you have target definitions from MRI and Spectra?
4. Do you have BDI/CDI for markets?
5. Are the markets listed IRI or Nielsen markets? (If so, do you have appropriate DMAs for these markets?)
6. Do you have ACV by market?
7. Do you know when consumer promotions are scheduled (particularly FSIs)?
8. Do you have category vs. brand seasonal sales and have compared both to spending?
9. Have you done alternative plans on media mixes?
10. What is role of advertising with the trade?
11. Is there a test component to the plan?
12. Do you know purchaser vs. user?
    - mom vs. kids

Source: FKM.

Exhibit 13.4

Media Checklist: B2B (Business-to-Business)

1. Do you have a clear understanding of the target?
    *   The right standard industrial classification code?
    *   The right job position?
    *   The decision process?
2. Is there any weighting to be done by target or industry groups?
3. When are decisions made?
    *   Are they ongoing or at a specific time of year?
4. Do they have a customer database of current and prospective customers?
    *   Should there be a retention program?
5. Do you have the industry or job universes to better understand coverage of media?
6. Are there any key trade shows to support or consider?
7. Is direct marketing part of the program?
8. Have you considered the Internet as part of the mix?
9. Are there any vehicles you can own?
10. Are premium positions in magazines worth the cost?
11. Is driving Web site traffic an important part of the plan?
12. Is there anything that you can test?

Source: FKM.

Exhibit 13.5

Pay Attention to the Numbers

In any analysis of a proposed advertising media plan, it is crucial to pay attention to the numbers—to determine whether they make sense and to see if they all add up correctly. This checklist may be of help.

1. Is the budget adequate? Is there enough money to accomplish all the objectives?
2. Does the target audience size make sense? Will it account for a sizeable portion of the target groups?
3. Are there enough media types to cover a diverse audience?
4. Are enough markets used to cover most of the country or most of the region in question?
5. Is there enough media weight to achieve sales goals? Enough markets? Adequate portion of coverage?
6. Are larger markets getting more of the media allocations?
7. Over the course of the campaign (e.g., for the coming year), will advertising frequency be sufficient?
8. Are the advertising units affordable and sensible?
9. Are reach, frequency, and impact balanced? For example, expensive units (bigger print advertisements, longer broadcast commercials, using color in print) cost more, which leaves less for reach and frequency. The corollary is that less expensive units will provide more money for more reach and frequency.
10. Are reach and frequency sensibly balanced?
11. Are expensive media (e.g., television) slated to receive larger budgetary allocations than less expensive media (e.g., outdoor)?

Chapter 14

Matching Media to the Total Brand Plan

As a brand manager, you are looking at an assortment of marketing activities in which media play a significant role. However, media cannot work in isolation. Due to the increased complexity of media and the continued fragmentation of audiences, more advertisers and agency media teams are approaching media in a broader manner.

There has been a rise in a new media planning model called *channel planning,* which offers a broader look at media than traditional media planning. Channel planning is also called *touchpoint planning* or *contact planning.*

Regardless of the name, there are some significant differences to this approach than traditional media planning. The first is that the media team will consider all consumer touchpoints (or interactions) with the brand and work to place them in a hierarchy. For example, the media team may examine how important a recommendation from a friend or family member is for the brand versus a message in a television ad. Or they may determine if in-store advertising, or promotions, or sponsorships of various events are of equal or differing importance. Traditionally, these analyses were made by the brand itself, or it was a siloed effort done by a specific marketing company such as a promotions agency or a public relations firm. While these same firms may still be executing the activities, the media team, along with the brand team, now has more say in the direction of these studies.

The second distinction between channel planning and traditional media planning is that it attempts to add some context to how the medium will deliver the ad. Channel planning offers the opportunity for input from the consumer and an evaluation of cost effectiveness when using a given medium. For example, if trust is a major consumer criterion for the brand, you will probably want to select media that the consumer feels are trustworthy. This may lead the media person down a different path than looking primarily at cost efficiencies.

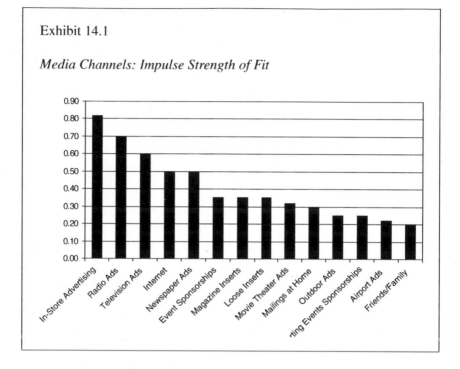

Exhibit 14.1

Media Channels: Impulse Strength of Fit

This type of media analysis has led to the use of both qualitative and quantitative methods for uncovering how consumers feel about different media as applied to different product categories. While this is usually custom research, traditional research companies such as Simmons Market Research Bureau (SMRB) and new companies such as Compose are developing syndicated tools that help media planners understand the link between a brand and various exposure opportunities.

Exhibit 14.1 illustrates how consumers view different media based on a brand's nature of being either a planned purchase or an impulse purchase. In this case, you are looking at how media are ranked in terms of delivering an impulse purchase. You will note that media touchpoints such as recommendations by a friend or family member are low on the list when a consumer is buying such an item; on the other hand, the point of sale is the top touchpoint. Therefore, a brand manager should direct a lot of energy toward developing effective point of sale material for an impulse brand.

Each brand and category has its own series of challenges when it comes to reaching the consumer. The point of this chapter is to help put all the marketing elements in some perspective.

For example, if you are in charge of a packaged-goods brand, media spending may represent only a third of the total dollars spent on behalf of the brand. You may be allocating significant dollars to trade promotions and another chunk of cash to consumer promotions. Both of these levers are more short-term-oriented than brand dollars. With the average tenure of a chief marketing officer now under 24 months, most brand managers don't have the luxury of a long-term view.

That being said, all your marketing dollars need to work together. Many times the way you schedule your media has an impact on other plan elements. In certain cases, you might use media in an unconventional manner to solve a trade problem. This might be to gain new distribution or to get more favorable facings for the brand within a store. Perhaps you need to enhance a consumer promotion and look to the media schedule as an ally to dial up this type of support. Regardless of your full brand plan, all of the elements must work together. The first step in this process is to look at a full year's activity plan.

Full Brand Plan

Just as a media plan has a flow chart that shows where the media weight is scheduled, a master flow chart of all the brand activities shows how they mesh.

If you are scheduling four coupon drops across the year, how does your media plan support those events? Perhaps you are cracking a new market and have a sampling program in progress. Is there media support for these events or are they a stand-alone activity? As a brand manager, you should avoid having a lot of small promotional activities with little impact; instead, you need to maximize your brand activities to have a meaningful impact on sales.

The same can be said of trade support. If you are discounting the price of your goods with a retailer and that retailer passes some of the savings on to the consumer, is that the only support you are going to offer? If you work in a large multibrand company, you may be working with other brand managers to develop cross-brand initiatives with the trade. You might be sponsoring other activities to secure more distribution. All these activities should work together with the media plan.

As mentioned earlier in discussing marketing objectives, you should bring the media planners in on the full brand plan. Obviously, there are trade-offs between these activities that are worthy of discussion. Just knowing all the issues will help the media planner craft a better media plan. (See Exhibit 14.2.)

Exhibit 14.2

Brand Planning Calendar for Magic Beans

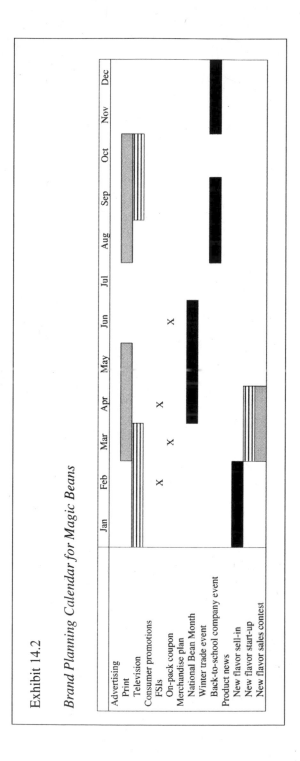

Consumer Promotions

The standard short-term consumer promotion is some sort of price incentive to induce consumers to try your product. This promotion may be a coupon, a rebate, a free sample, or a buy-one-get-one-free offer.

Whatever promotional tactic you might be implementing, you need to match your tactic to the media plan. Let's say that you are scheduling a coupon that runs in a free-standing insert (FSI), which is distributed in the Sunday newspaper. How do you schedule media support around it?

Research shows that if you use media to lead into a coupon drop, the redemption of that coupon is greatly enhanced. So creating some awareness in other media can have a positive impact on your consumer promotion, in this case, the FSI. It is important to recognize this impact when you budget for coupon redemption.

For example, suppose that you distributed 1 million coupons in the FSI at 30 cents apiece. That is a total liability of $300,000 if everyone redeems a coupon (not counting handling expenses). The difference between a 3 percent redemption rate and a 5 percent redemption rate is $6,000 ($15,000 – $9,000). That isn't a big deal, but if you were doing a national drop to 80 million households, then the difference becomes $480,000. Now that is some serious change.

It is important to understand the dynamics of media support when applying it to consumer promotions.

Consumer Events

Another way of reaching your customer is with consumer events. An event can be as simple as setting up a product demonstration in a retail location for sampling purposes or as complex as sponsoring a series of concerts by a well-known artist. There are also events that you manufacture yourself.

For example, Oscar Mayer has had a Wienermobile travel around to various markets, creating a buzz for the brand while giving out merchandise and, of course, coupons for Oscar Mayer wieners. Oscar Mayer created its own event, and it has become a part of the brand. Other brands do similar things.

So how does a media plan support some nomads running around the country in the Wienermobile? It can in a number of ways. Perhaps your media plan calls for radio stations in every market to hype the Wienermobile. They set up at the grocery store and hold a live remote promoting the event. Or you may develop a series of newspaper advertisements to promote the Wienermobile's whereabouts. The point is that media do not have to support an event, but they certainly can.

Sometimes, the media themselves can create and hold events. *Southern Living* magazine started a series of cooking schools that constitute a traveling road show, reaching into many of the magazine's markets. Based on a certain commitment to advertise in the magazine, your brand can be a part of these shows and even be featured in various recipes. It is a grassroots way to gain valuable trial and support. Many other publications and other media sponsor similar types of events.

With the melding of radio station ownership and recording labels under the same ownership, there is an increasing amount of product sponsorship of artists who are promoted at the concert level and cross-promoted on radio stations. Beer manufacturers are very involved in these types of product events.

Whether you have an icon like the Wienermobile or have purchased a media vehicle that offers a ready-made event, consumer events need to be treated like any other part of the plan. The media plan must at the minimum recognize the event and possibly be tied in to it.

Changing Nature of the Trade

Within the last decade, there has been a power shift between the retailer and the manufacturer. It used to be that the retail channels were very fragmented. This was particularly true in the grocery business, where nearly every market had a strong local grocery. The same can be said for many other retailing categories as well.

Those days are now well behind us. The relentless growth of Wal-Mart in the mass merchandise as well as the grocery and pharmacy arenas has led to a rapid consolidation of the retail sector. No longer is sales management calling on disparate bunches of retailers. Now manufacturers must present a major retail chain with well-crafted programs.

Most sophisticated retailers have category managers who basically run a business within the overall retail business. These specialists are in charge of a category of merchandise—say, frozen foods, or detergents, or dairy items. Your role is to help the category managers grow their business by bringing consumers to their category through your marketing plan.

The media plan plays into this strategy in a number of ways. First of all, it is presented to the category manager along with the rest of the brand plan to help gain favorable shelf space in the stores. Secondly, the category managers are consumers, too, so they are certainly influenced by your advertising.

Dealing with the Trade

In presenting a media plan to a retailer, the objective is to look as big as possible. You want to appear as if you are supporting your brand as strongly as you can. To accomplish this, you need to show the retailer your "boxcar" numbers. For example, if you are scheduling broadcast television and/or cable support, you might show the retailer your household rating points instead of target rating points; if you have 100 target rating points a week, that may convert to about 150 household rating points. You can also describe the media plan using total advertising impressions: "This plan reaches 90 million households an average of 20 times for a total of 1.8 billion impressions."

You may think that this approach is just playing games. To some extent, it is, but in order to execute your plan, you must get your product onto the shelf. Because this is a common sell-in tactic, you may want to play the same game as your competition.

The point of this discussion is that the trade is your first audience. Without it, you have a product without a way of gaining consumers. It is crucial that you convince category managers that your brand will help them achieve the goal of growing the category. The category manager will ultimately judge you on your ability to bring more consumers to the category and to achieve a profitable level of sales.

Trade Feather

To ensure that the retailer is well aware of the support you are putting behind your brand, you may consider scheduling an increased amount of advertising in the retail headquarters market. This is known in the media world as providing a "trade feather"—that is, tickling the trade in its home market. In this case, you are aiming at the category managers, not the usual consumer target. Most category managers in the grocery and pharmacy world are men, while the consumer is typically a woman. So you may place your commercials on the television or radio news, you may schedule a special insert to run in that market, or even have a billboard strategically placed so category managers see it on the way to work.

The airwaves of Springfield, Missouri, which is the designated market area (DMA) for Wal-Mart, are strewn with manufacturers catering to this giant. Similarly, the airwaves in Boise, Idaho, the home of Albertson's food chain, and Atlanta, which is headquarters for the home improvement retailer Home Depot, support these major retail outlets. This is advertising intended to reach the product buyers at large retail headquarters.

So the media plan can be crafted to help the sales process. Sometimes the most important media placement is the one that reaches the category manager who will decide whether your brand will be exposed to the consumer market or not.

The media effort is a part of the total brand plan. It can be an important part of the puzzle on its own, but it can be even more valuable when it works in concert with the other brand tools. With the versatility of media today, you need to consider media in untraditional roles, whether as a part of a promotional plan or in helping the brand gain more shelf space.

Chapter 15

Developing Test Plans

Every brand is looking for the optimum way to allocate its funds. Some brands spend a lot on advertising; others do not. Some use television; others use print. Because every brand is unique, it is important to develop a base of knowledge that, over time, guides the brand's support. That is why many brands develop test plans; it is a relatively safe and low-cost way to learn what works and what doesn't for your brand.

Test marketing is the use of controlled tests in one or more geographic areas to gather information about the brand, customers, and competitors. There are two basic reasons to test-market. The first is to gain knowledge about a new product or line extension in a limited area before rolling it out nationally. The second is to test different marketing-mix strategies for an existing brand. These strategies can include a media-weight test, a media-mix test, a comparison of different copy strategies, or a test of a different blend of advertising-to-trade support.

Test marketing gives the brand management a lot of opportunities to learn as well as to fine-tune the brand strategy. It helps reduce the odds of failure for a future strategy, and it can lead the brand to a bolder strategy. Success depends on setting up an effective and representative test-market situation.

Establishing a worthwhile test-market scenario requires the proper research structure, appropriate test markets, and the ability to act on the information on a broad scale.

Guidelines for Test Marketing

It is a terrible mistake to believe that you have an appropriate test only to find that something muddied the water and you now can't read it or rely on it. It is important to set up the proper structure for having test markets that are reliable and projectable, that have the ability to broadcast to a broader area.

While there are no hard-and-fast rules about what makes for a proper

Table 15.1

Test Marketing Standards

2+ Test markets
1+ Control market
Geographically dispersed
Demographically representative of the United States
Test length at least 6 months
Weight levels tests at 50 percent ±

---

test, there are some standards that over the years have served brand managers well. The following standards are recommended for test marketing (See Table 15.1). There should be a minimum of two test markets in addition to a control market for most tests. If you are introducing a new brand, you would likely want three or four test markets in order to protect yourself from a regional bias.

You should select markets that are geographically dispersed. If you concentrate your entire test in a certain region and the regional economy tanks, then you have an unreadable test.

Markets should be representative of the United States, unless there is a specific ethnic or demographic skew to your brand. Then you would want markets that mirror the category in which you compete. You also want the markets that you select to cover 3 percent or more of the country, so you'll have a sizable population base that has good projectability.

Most tests should run for at least six months. For most brands that have a four-week purchase cycle, a six-month test would allow for six complete purchase cycles and 26 individual data points that allow for statistical comparison to a baseline. If possible, it is desirable to schedule a test for 12 months to offer greater numbers of data points so that your test period can be statistically validated. If you have a product with a longer purchase cycle than four weeks, then you should consider testing for longer than a year in order to be able to read and trust the results.

If you are testing media-weight levels, you should look to increase or decrease the weight level by a minimum of 50 percent. If you adjust it less than this amount, you run the risk of not having data on which you can rely.

Selecting Test Markets

One of the most important elements in test marketing is selecting the right markets in which to test. For example, if you are testing a new baby formula and picked Fort Myers, Florida, where more than 50 percent of the popula-

Table 15.2

Examples of Top Test Markets

Designated market area	Market rank	Percentage of United States
Oklahoma City	45	0.597
Louisville, KY	50	0.574
Tulsa	60	0.466
Toledo	68	0.406
Des Moines	72	0.376
Omaha	78	0.363
Syracuse	80	0.352
Rochester, NY	77	0.364
Spokane	79	0.357
Madison, WI	86	0.327
Colorado Springs	94	0.284

Source: Nielsen Media Research. U.S. TV Household Estimates.

tion is over the age of 55, that might not pan out for you. The market must reflect the population of the United States or whatever the population base is in which your brand operates.

The second aspect to a test market is to select a market that is neither too small nor too big. Typically, a test market should be no less than 0.2 percent but no more than 2.0 percent of the United States. This usually translates to markets that range from 30 to 150 of the top 210 designated market areas. Table 15.2 shows some of the more popular test markets.

If you select a market that is too small, it might not have the appropriate number of media outlets to translate your test plan. If it is too big, it is not very cost-efficient. Who wants to test a plan in New York, where media rates are sky-high? As we discussed before, once you are in a few of the top 10 markets, you may have the media equivalent of a national brand.

Media Requirements

A test market must have a variety of media outlets available. It should be representative of the normal market. A market should have at least four television stations, which are basically the Big Four networks. Cable penetration should be no more than 10 percent above or below the national average; if it is outside this range, then you run the risk of a skewed viewing environment. The market should have a good range of radio stations covering a variety of formats. It should also have a dominant local newspaper that includes a daily and a Sunday edition. The Sunday newspaper should contain Sunday supplements and free-standing inserts. It is essential that the medium you want to test is contained in the test market.

Another aspect of test markets is their degree of media isolation. For example, San Angelo, Texas, receives more than 20 percent of its television viewing from Dallas/Fort Worth. You wouldn't want to purchase both San Angelo and Dallas stations for a test market. This is known as *spill-in,* when television signals from one market may be seen in another market.

Conversely, you don't want to air your commercials in one market and have them seen in another market where consumers can't get your product. You don't want to have consumers coming to your future retailing partner looking for a product that is not on the shelf. Television spill-in or spill-out should be restricted to less than 15 percent.

Marketing Criteria

If you are developing a test market for an existing product, you will want to find markets in which it makes sense to test. First, you want a market where you have solid distribution; it makes little sense to do a heavy spend test if you are not in 50 percent of the distribution outlets in the market. Once you have the proper distribution, then you should find markets that have average sales characteristics. If you have a 70 percent market share, the chance of pushing it up 20 percent, to 84 percent market share, is a lot less likely than picking a market where you start with only a 20 percent market share.

Use your brand and category indexes (BDI and CDI) to help establish the criteria. For a test market, you should keep within a range of 115 to 85, or plus or minus 15 percentage points, from the average. The goal is to keep the markets as typical as possible, assuming that your test is designed to be rolled out nationally.

BehaviorScan Markets

For consumer packaged-goods (CPG) brands, one popular method of test marketing is to use Information Resources Inc.'s BehaviorScan test-marketing method. BehaviorScan uses a household panel in discrete designated marketing areas (DMAs) to measure the impact of advertising and actual product-sales movement of the test brand.

Respondents in the panel use a wand to scan their grocery and drug purchases. These same respondents also have their television viewing metered so you can understand their viewing behavior. In addition, respondents are profiled regarding their other media habits as well as their purchase behavior.

BehaviorScan has markets that cut across the country. You can choose from markets such as Cedar Rapids, Iowa; Midland, Texas; and Pittsfield, Massachusetts. When you choose to use a BehaviorScan test, obviously the test-market criteria are already taken care of. If you elect to do your own study, then stick to the criteria in the previous section.

Test-Market Translations

When you are developing a test plan, you should start with how your plan will ultimately be executed. For example, testing a plan that might translate to a $50 million national plan if you know that you can't afford such a plan is a waste of time. If your goal is to be a national brand, start with the objective of how you would execute the tested plan on a national basis; if your goal is to be a regional brand, focus on executing the plan on a system-wide basis.

Assuming that your goal is to be a national brand or to implement your test on a national basis, let's review the techniques for doing just that. There are two commonly used techniques for translating national media plans into local test plans. The two techniques are called "Little USA" and "As It Falls."

"Little USA," sometimes called "Little America," assigns each test market to receive the average national rating-point levels. This technique assumes that the local market will behave similarly to the whole United States. So if a national media plan calls for 100 network television rating points and 100 magazine rating points, then each test market would be assigned those weight levels. The plan at the local level is a replication of the plan at the national level.

The "As It Falls" method is a bit different from the "Little USA" approach. In the "As It Falls" method, each test market's media delivery is based on what that delivery would be if the plan were to be implemented nationally. So if the national plan calls for 100 network television rating points and your test market normally delivers 10 percent above the average in terms of network delivery, then the test market would receive 110 rating points. The purpose of the "As It Falls" method is to replicate as precisely as possible the actual national plan that would be implemented.

There are reasons to select one method over the other. "Little USA" is best used when the advertiser is testing a new brand and has no benchmark category sales data available on a local market level. In this case, you want to understand the performance of the product and not necessarily the media variation. On the other hand, if a brand has a good amount of historical sales data, then the "As It Falls" method is preferable because it is closer to what will actually happen once the plan is implemented nationally. You may want to compromise if you find that the "As It Falls" test markets produce abnormally low or high rating-point delivery compared to the national plan. Then you either go to a "Little USA" method or reexamine your test markets.

Translating National Media to the Local Level

You've figured out what you want to test. The media group has developed the perfect national plan. You've selected your test markets. Now you have to take that hypothetical national media plan and execute it in the test markets. In doing so, you need to make some media decisions. Unfortunately, the process is not as simple as taking one plan and executing it. National media and local media are different. Each medium has its own nuances. Getting the stars to align takes some work. Let's examine the four major national media, starting with network television.

The biggest difference between scheduling commercials in network television versus spot or local television is that network purchases are usually made within an actual program while spot purchases are made between the programs. For example, if you use CBS's *Two and a Half Men,* your commercial will run within the actual program, either at the ten-minute or twenty-minute commercial break after this show begins. Spot television, however, offers commercials at the program break, so your commercial would air between *Two and a Half Men* and the following program. Why is this important? Research shows that retention of commercials at the between-program break drops 20 to 30 percent compared to commercials within a program. Therefore, you may want to boost your test plan to compensate for this inequity.

Unlike network television, 15-second commercials are immediately preemptable in spot television. This means that unless a local station has another advertiser running a 15-second unit in the same program that you are, your commercial will not air. There are few natural breaks for 15-second commercials on a local basis, so the chances of your commercial not running can be great. As a result, you may want to schedule 30-second commercials on a spot basis to guard against being bumped off the air.

Cable television is very difficult to translate to a local market. Many local cable operators sell advertising only on selective channels, which may not be the ones you would purchase. Even on those channels that they do sell, they may offer only broad rotation schedules so you cannot pick the time you want. In some areas, local cable operators may not sell advertising. Local cable is problematic at best. If national cable is a part of an overall plan, you should consider purchasing that test weight on over-the-air television. Local early fringe, late fringe, and/or weekend times can be good substitutes for cable weight.

Network radio translates well to the local level. In radio, it is important to ensure that whatever station format you plan on using nationally, you end up purchasing locally. The only other nuance to radio is the cost implications of 60-second commercials versus 30-second commercials. Usually, :30s are half the price of :60s nationally, yet many local stations charge the same for :60s and :30s locally.

Magazine placement has its own set of issues as well. Depending upon the publication, it may not have a large enough circulation to offer a test-market edition. Most large circulation publications such as *Good Housekeeping, Time,* and *TV Guide* offer very detailed local editions. But if your strategy is to be in more "niche" publications such as *Chili Pepper,* then you are going to run into problems. All you can do is to find publications that are similar in nature to what you plan on scheduling.

The other major issue with magazines is the type of unit that can be scheduled in a test-market edition of a national publication. Because publications must actually make a mechanical plate change in the printing process to accommodate your advertisement, they usually allow only full-page advertisements to be in a test-market edition. So if your test plan calls for checkerboard advertisements or a fractional unit, you may want to rethink your test. A checkerboard is scheduling quarter-page ads in each of the four corners of a two-page spread; fractional units are anything less than a full page, such as a two-thirds–page or half-page unit. Regardless of your creative wishes, you must use some practical sense when testing in magazines.

Developing test plans does take some serious thought. You need to have your objectives honed with the understanding that what you test can actually be rolled out. Then, select the proper test markets and develop your test translation. Finally, work the local plan so that it fits the national plan as closely as possible.

Tactical Testing

This chapter has focused on developing classical test-market plans typically used with CPG brands. The basic tenets of this type of planning can apply to any brand situation regardless of category. However, you don't have to develop classic test-market scenarios to have a valid test.

As a brand manager, you should always be looking at ways to improve your advertising and media program. Learning what works or doesn't work provides a golden opportunity to further your brand's cause in the marketplace. There are plenty of areas to do small tactical tests that can reap big rewards: all you have to do is isolate the variable to be tested and have test and control markets.

For example, suppose that you are a retail brand that relies on weekly inserts to drive traffic to your store. You could test if you want your ad to be inserted in the weekday or Sunday newspaper. Or you could see if paid newspapers outperformed free distribution papers. A home accessories retail chain recently ran a test where they changed their insert drop from Sunday to Thursday. They found that their sales had no change by moving the date but they saved nearly 30% on their media costs since the Sunday paper had a higher cost per thousand than the daily, plus it distributed more copies. By doing this small tactical test, this retailer saved millions of dollars for the company.

The same is true for business-to-business marketing. You can isolate a market or a particular job title to do a test. One business-to-business marketer had a publication sort his database with their circulation. For the customers that they had in common, he sent one message; to the prospects, he sent another. This led to an increase in both new customer acquisition as well as retention of existing customers.

If you have an online component to your marketing plan, you are in a constant state of testing. Most online campaigns are built similar to direct marketing campaigns with message, creative, offer, and media testing all available. It is like being in a test kitchen for a restaurant chain. Just about anything that can be thought of can be tested in the online arena. Online media can be an effective laboratory to test ideas before rolling them out to offline media.

Whether you are developing classic test-market scenarios or you want to understand how one media vehicle performs, test marketing should be a part of any media plan. As a brand manager, you want to continually add to the brand's knowledge base. Test marketing is one consistent method of doing just that.

Chapter 16

What to Look for in Media Execution

You have approved the brand's media plan. All the effort you have put into crafting a solid marketing plan and translating that into advertising and subsequently into media strategy should make you feel pretty good about yourself. But your work is not finished. If the media plan is not executed properly, all the hard work that went into the front end of the process is for naught.

Execution of the media plan is not as simple as ordering off the menu. In this case, you may know what you want, but you are going to have to negotiate well to get it. Purchasing media is like purchasing in the stock market: there are buyers and sellers; the market ebbs and flows; timing is crucial to get the best deal. Most media plans, then, have some areas of compromise as they are negotiated.

How to purchase media could be a book unto itself. It is important that you understand what goes into a buy so you can evaluate it properly. Each medium has its own set of nuances and areas to evaluate. Let's take a look at each medium and how to evaluate the plan execution.

Broadcast Network Television

Every spring, usually around May or June, there is a ritual that seems akin to some odd form of mating dance. That is the network *up-front* buying season. Network television is purchased in one of three ways: in the up-front market, in the scatter market, or opportunistically.

The network up-front is driven by the networks, not by the advertisers. The up-front crosses two calendar years, beginning in the fourth quarter of one year and going through the third quarter of the following year. It coincides with the introduction of new prime-time programs that kick off in the fall. To be a part of the up-front market, you typically need to be advertising in the same daypart for two or more quarters.

There are some big advantages to being an up-front advertiser. The first is that you get first choice of the best programming. Networks sell around 75 percent or more of their commercial inventories in the up-front market, so it may be slim pickings afterward. The second advantage is that you usually get a lower cost per thousand (CPM; the cost to deliver your message to 1,000 people) by being in the up-front market. The third advantage is that you negotiate ratings guarantees. Thus, if your schedule isn't delivering the 100 rating points that you purchased and were promised, the network is obligated to add units to the schedule at no additional charge to make up the difference. You can also negotiate options out of inventory with no penalties. For example, if you have made a purchase running over three quarters of the year, the first quarter you have a schedule in is 100 percent firm, but the succeeding quarters may have 50 percent "out" options. A 50 percent out option means that at a certain point (usually at least three months prior to the airdate) you can cancel up to half of your network schedule. If your brand suddenly hits a distribution snag or it isn't performing as well as expected, you can recoup some of your advertising dollars. This change is aptly called *seeking relief.*

The *scatter market* is scheduled on a quarter-by-quarter basis, which allows you to negotiate for the upcoming quarter. The benefits of scatter are that you have more flexibility with your advertising media dollars, so—if the market is soft—you may be able to pick up a good deal. But you do not typically get ratings guarantees or "out" options in scatter; your purchase is 100 percent firm.

Opportunistic is a fancy word for buying at the last minute. The upside of this approach is that you might get a fabulous deal if a network has inventory that it needs to unload. The downside is that you might not get what you want or you may have to pay a premium to get it.

Now you have made your buy. What do you look at? You should check to see whether the rating points that you planned were actually purchased. You may want to verify that you are on target with your budget. You will want to review the type of programming that you purchased to see if it is in line with your goals (See Table 16.1).

Many companies have a *program hit list* (see Table 16.2), which is a list of programs that they deem too sexually explicit or violent. Companies do not want advertisements for their brand to appear during the broadcast of these shows. This concern is something to communicate to the advertising agency before the plan is executed.

One more item to look for on your buy is a sore point in the network purchase process, an integration fee. Each network commercial unit is charged an integration fee that typically ranges from $200 to $500 for the privilege of being placed in the program. This fee originated when the networks had

Table 16.1

Plan vs. Purchase, Network TV Buy—Women 18 to 49

	Plan		Purchase/index to plan			
Dayparts	Target rating points	In million dollars	Target rating points	Index	In million dollars	Index
Morning	400	2.400	420	105	2.300	96
Daytime	600	2.700	650	108	2.800	104
Prime time	800	8.500	750	94	8.500	100
	1,800	13.600	1,820	101	13.600	100

Table 16.2

Sample Hit List/Programs to Avoid

Judge Judy
Cops
Dirty Sexy Money
The Simpsons
All My Children

to integrate each commercial into a program manually. That is certainly not the case today, but the charge has held up over time. Don't be surprised to see it on your bill.

Cable Television

Network cable purchasing is very similar to that of network television. You can purchase cable in the up-front or scatter markets. You can negotiate ratings guarantees and options in the up-front market. You purchase programs on a network, just like on network television.

The big difference between network cable and network broadcast television is that cable does not charge commercial integration fees. In fact, when CNN first began selling advertising in the early 1980s, it was sold on the basis that a commercial unit on *Headline News* cost less than a network integration fee. At that time, the cost for a 30-second commercial on *Headline News* was around $400, a small fraction of today's rates.

The other major difference between network broadcast television and cable is in the number of households that receive the signal. Nearly 100 percent of all homes receive network signals, but only about 75 percent subscribe to cable. Each cable operation has its own distribution because cable operators pay for the programming. CNN may be in nearly all cable homes, but a specialized network like Food Network may be in only half. So you should check the total number of households that each network is in when you review the buy.

You can review the same criteria as you did for network buys. Did the purchase meet plan? Was it on budget and are the programs acceptable?

Spot Television

Spot television is purchased typically on a quarter-year basis, although it can be negotiated for longer periods. Unlike network television, spot television does not guarantee its ratings, so there is much more maintenance involved in the spot market than the network market.

Just as for network television and cable, you will want to see whether the purchase met the plan goals for rating delivery and budget. In screening programs, it is important to remember that most spot purchases are at the hour and half-hour break positions between programs. Therefore, the buyer may not purchase *The Oprah Winfrey Show,* but your commercial could well be placed leading into that program or leading out of it. If this is a concern, you should review your guidelines with the buyer prior to placement.

Network Radio

Network radio purchasing is much like that of network television, with an up-front and scatter method of buying. Unlike network television, though, there is no real season for radio; therefore, you can purchase radio time on a calendar-year basis or whatever your brand's fiscal year may be.

When purchasing network radio, you are buying a blanket of stations across the country. They are typically organized by format, so you can buy all country music stations, all news stations, all easy listening, or all pop and rock. However, each network has a mix of stations that perform at varying strengths in each market. So unlike buying a network television program like *60 Minutes,* you are purchasing hundreds of different morning shows on various radio stations across the country. You should check the station selection to see whether it fits with the brand's strength, market by market.

Network radio also sells what is called long-form programming. You have probably heard of *American Top 40,* a prime example of a long-form program. Typically, long-form programs are over an hour in length. There are a variety of shows that are syndicated through these same radio stations that are on the traditional network schedules.

The tricky part of network radio is to make sure that the individual market radio station support is good where you need it. If you purchased 50 rating points but you only get five in New York, and New York accounts for 20 percent of your sales, your buy is probably not a good one. Once the buy is done, do the normal checking of budget and ratings relative to goal, but dig a bit deeper to understand the geographical impact of those ratings.

Spot Radio

Spot radio, like spot television, is purchased typically on a quarterly basis. Local radio is just that—very local. The top format or station in one market may not be on top in the next market. Local station personalities help to drive a station's popularity. If your brand is very local, you might consider taking advantage of a radio team's good reputation.

In looking at a radio purchase, it is important to look at the listener composition of each station. Say you are trying to reach young women ages 25 to 34: there may be a station in the market that has more than half its audience composed of this target. Have a station rank pulled for the top-ranked stations in the market for your audience, as well as for the highest-ranked audience composition. Those are the two factors, along with cost, that determine a radio purchase.

Otherwise, assess the rating delivery and the budget against your plan, just as with all other media.

Magazines

Magazine advertisements are usually purchased on an annual basis to get the best deal possible. Magazines do have published rate cards, but the trend in recent years is to negotiate rates and other items. The rate card is a good starting place, but you should set up a negotiation period as well.

Most agencies send out requests for proposals (RFPs) to the various magazines that they are considering, giving them the buying specifications. This process, which is similar to television negotiation, takes some time to complete.

Also, publishing groups now own many publications, so you may have an opportunity to develop a group combination rate. You will want to check the type of publications that are purchased. Do they reach your audience? Are they large-reach vehicles or smaller niche publications? Does your strategy call for a mix of these types of vehicles? Those are the questions to consider when looking at a magazine plan.

In negotiating magazines, your rates are pegged to the contract that you sign. If you opt out of some of the commitment, you may suffer what is called a short rate. A short rate is a penalty for not fulfilling your contract level; in some cases, it can be substantial.

Newspapers

Newspapers are one of the most flexible of all media. You can place an advertisement on Tuesday and have it run that Thursday. Newspaper space can be purchased weekly or annually. If you know your plan ahead of time, you can negotiate a better contract than by placing it at the last minute.

Like magazines, newspapers have contracts that are based on the dollars you have committed to spend. If you don't spend that amount, you will suffer a short rate. If you go substantially over the amount, you might get a rebate. Getting a rebate or money back might sound like a good thing. However, most advertisers would rather have had that money to invest in more advertising during their schedule rather than getting back a check after it has run.

The keys to look for in newspaper placement are what section your ad is going to be in and what day of the week it is running. Most newspapers have special sections that run on certain days, such as best food day, when all the grocery stores run their circulars. Weekday placements usually cost less than Sunday because circulation is typically lower on the weekday than the weekend.

Out-of-Home Media

Outdoor media are typically bought on a monthly basis in terms of showings. A showing consists of a specific number of billboards that represent a daily coverage percent of the market's traffic. For example, a 25 showing is equivalent to reaching 25 percent of your target market on a daily basis. Showing sizes can range from 10 to 100 but are typically in increments of 25 such as 25, 50, 75, and 100.

To calculate a showing size or just to understand how many consumers may see a single billboard, outdoor companies provide a traffic audit called a *daily effective circulation* (DEC). This DEC count is the estimated number of adults who have the opportunity to see the billboard.

For 14×48 billboards, the large ones on the major arteries, you can buy a permanent board, or a rotary program. A permanent board is a specific location which is usually sold on an annual basis. A rotary program consists of a pool of locations which rotate every two or three months depending upon the outdoor operator. Rotaries are sold in showings with commitments of three, six, nine, and twelve months.

For surface streets or specific parts of town, you can elect to purchase a poster showing. Posters come in 30 sheets for roadways and 10 sheets for more pedestrian-oriented viewing. These also are purchased in showing sizes.

Alternative out-of-home media such as pump toppers (signs at gas stations), grocery cart ads, airport transit, bus advertising, taxi cab signage, and so on are all purchased on the same premise as traditional outdoor. Typically, these media develop showing sizes and have some basis for arriving at an estimate of opportunities to view the advertising.

The key to outdoor advertising is pretty simple. It is like real estate: location, location, location. If you are committing a good sum of funds to outdoor, you will likely want an agency representative to "ride the market" and pick the appropriate locations for the brand. In the cases of nontraditional out-of-home, it may be necessary to gain specific installation dates so that your campaign is launched when you want it to be. Most outdoor companies prepare a showing within 15 days, but weather can stretch this time frame. If you have a timely message, work with the agency and outdoor company on a plan of action to meet your demands.

Online

Online advertising can take a lot of forms. There are response campaigns not unlike other areas of direct response advertising. Among these are *brand campaigns* and *search engine marketing*. Let's tackle each one of these areas because there are specific nuances to each.

Purchasing ads for brand campaigns is done on a CPM basis similar to that of other media. Impressions are estimated for the ads that are served to the specific sites or search engines that you request. Although there are standards set by the Interactive Advertising Bureau on creative specifications, there is truly no "one size fits all" online media. This is particularly true in terms of rich media, where some sites may not have the bandwidth to accommodate a strong video-based ad. One key to execution of a brand campaign is to make sure that creative and media have communicated so that you don't miss an opportunity to be on the right site due to the nonacceptance of the creative unit.

Once you begin to get the diagnostics of your campaign, you should be prepared to have various creative units in the queue—particularly if you find something that works well or doesn't perform well. Likewise, you may consider holding a contingency fund of dollars for the media execution until you see what is working and what isn't working. In tracking a brand campaign, you can measure the standard metrics (generally, the click-through rates); however, you may want to consider a more performance-based study conducted by Millward Brown called Dynamic Logic. Dynamic Logic polls their online panel to determine who has seen your ad and the brand recognition that it has obtained. If you are more interested in brand building than specific response, then this is a metric you should consider.

If you are looking for a specific response, then build your plan around those metrics. Many online campaigns have strict return on investment (ROI) criteria built into each media plan. For example, if you are selling laptops and you know that your cost per sale needs to be less than $30 for you to make money, you can negotiate with the media to pay for impressions based on this type of metric. It is important to sit down and talk with the interactive media planner to determine the best course of action that you want to take when evaluating a direct response type of campaign.

Search engine marketing (SEM) or keyword search accounts for the largest portion of media spent online and is very different from other forms of media. It is done on a bid basis, where you submit a bid to be listed when a certain keyword is searched. For example, if you are an auto insurance company, you may pay $100 for the keyword "auto insurance." However, unlike other media, you don't pay for the keyword unless someone actually clicks on your ad. So, if your ad pops up and nothing happens, no harm, no foul. However, if you have a popular search area such as travel or insurance, you can spend a lot of money very quickly in this area. Therefore, many advertisers will have a ceiling on the amount that they will spend during a certain period of time until they can understand the return on investment that SEM is providing them.

The next level of search engine marketing is called search engine optimization (SEO). There are interactive marketing and media companies that run sophisticated analytics to optimize an advertiser's search engine dollars. Companies like these are constantly monitoring the search campaign to adjust it on the fly and to develop algorithms that can optimize the search process. For brands where SEM is a big aspect of their business, SEO is a vital aspect of this activity. (See Exhibit 16.1.)

Regardless of the type of online activity you are engaged in, there are metrics that will allow you to determine its effectiveness. Most advertisers test various media and creative for a couple of weeks to determine what is working and what isn't working for the brand.

Post Buys

This brings us to a key part of the media process—accountability. You can order the right program, buy space in the right publication, or schedule on a Web site, but did your commercial actually run as requested? You will want to look at a post-buy analysis for each medium after the schedule has been placed.

Exhibit 16.1

Share of Online Dollars

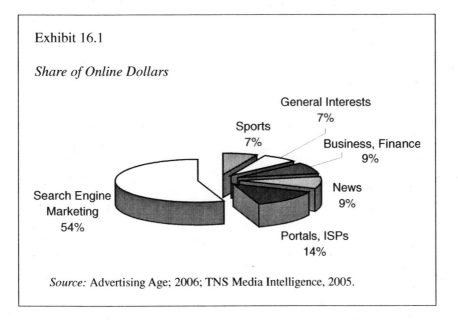

Source: Advertising Age; 2006; TNS Media Intelligence, 2005.

In the television and cable area, ratings are forecast for each program to air. Once it airs, ratings data indicate how it actually performed. Put these two pieces of data together and you have a post buy. You want to see if what the buyer said would happen actually did.

Broadcast post buys are usually made on a quarterly basis, when the new rating data are available and the invoices from the stations have been compared to the original purchase. If the ratings do not match up to the buy, then the buyer should go back to that station and recover bonus weight to make up for that underdelivery at a future date.

With Nielsen meter data, media buyers are typically evaluating performance on a station on a weekly basis, so they can head off any shortfalls immediately. They also make sure that a schedule airs as ordered. Stations may preempt your commercial if they have to run a political advertisement or if they receive an order from an advertiser willing to pay a much higher rate for the commercial time. So the post buy is a proof point to ensure that the brand is getting what it has paid for.

Other media receive grade cards as well. Radio is similar to television in that it is "posted" on what was scheduled to air versus what actually aired. Magazines are graded according to a positioning report; media planners evaluate where the advertisement was placed in the magazine to see if it appeared as requested.

Newspapers provide a tear sheet, which is proof that the advertisement ran. Media planners evaluate the position of the advertisement on the page and on what page or section it appeared.

Merchandising

One other aspect of media negotiation is receiving something extra for the dollars that your brand is spending, which is typically called merchandising or added value. It is something above the actual media time or space that has some value for the brand. A radio station may offer to do a live remote in the parking lot of a grocery store for your brand if the station receives a certain amount of money. A television station may run a contest on your brand's behalf. Or a magazine might feature your brand in a recipe or throw a party for some of your key clients.

All of these are extra items that can make a media buy more than just meeting some stringent set of numbers. If the extras are special, a buyer may bring to your attention a complete program that you might not get otherwise.

As you go through any media buy, always look for the merchandising aspects of the buy. What are those extra items that you received? Is there a vehicle that is so aggressive that it might deserve extra money? These are among the issues that media planners and buyers wrestle with as they complete a purchase on your behalf.

Cross-Platform Deals

The rapid consolidation of media companies has produced new opportunities to purchase media time and space. These are called cross-platform deals. The cross-platform deal is the ability to purchase multiple properties from a single large media company. There are two advantages to this type of negotiation: The first is gaining cost concessions. The second is gaining synergy among the properties.

For example, you might approach Time Warner to purchase a schedule on CNN, followed by a print ad in *Time* magazine, and schedule a contest on AOL with the winner to be honored at a CNN dinner. The possibilities are certainly there for some creative ways to make your budget come to life.

With more and more media properties offering a mix of traditional as well as online properties, it is important to evaluate media opportunities in a wide variety of ways. Sometimes a cross-platform deal doesn't make sense, and frankly, many media companies still have a difficult time executing such a deal, since it involves gaining the cooperation of competing sales organizations. But it is certainly a method that should be discussed for the brand to see if it offers some form of opportunity.

Chapter 17

Effects, Tools, and Trends

Smart marketers want to know whether their advertising is effective. Because advertising media make up the biggest portion of the advertising expense, the impact of advertising media is an especially important factor.

Media accountability has always been an issue. Historically, media accountability has centered on the delivery of each medium. For print vehicles, that meant ensuring that the circulation that was paid for was actually delivered. Within the past few years, there have been various scandals in the newspaper industry involving large major daily newspapers, such as the *Dallas Morning News,* giving advertisers false circulation and readership information. This problem certainly has been rectified, but it does point out the continued burden of media accountability that is required in the industry.

The broadcast industry also has accountability issues. In the television and cable industry, schedules are agreed upon in the future and then posted after airing to determine whether advertisers have achieved their delivery goals. Stations will provide bonus weight if a schedule does not meet delivery goals. With Nielsen Media Research providing an ongoing stream of metered household measurement, the level of accountability is growing. In 2006, a new layer of accountability began in broadcast—a movement from program ratings as currency to actual commercial ratings. Advertisers clamored for more detailed information on the actual viewing of their commercials rather than just program rating information. Nielsen's measurement service, capable of providing minute-by-minute ratings, could account for any viewer slippage from watching the program to the commercial. So, the pressure was put on the industry to conform to a new standard of accountability in audience delivery.

Radio is also going through growing pains on accountability. Diary measurement systems of radio have not allowed advertisers the same degree of accountability as in television. In 2006, the Arbitron radio ratings service rolled out its version of the television meter system. The portable ratings meter from Arbitron is a pager device worn by the respondent that captures encoded audio signals. Tested in Philadelphia and Houston, the device offers advertisers a much more robust audience measurement tool that provides more current and detailed information. As this book is being written, other research companies are challenging Arbitron with their versions of electronic measurement.

The increasing emphasis on media audience accountability has given rise to a new breed of media auditing companies. Pioneered in the United Kingdom and now a growing factor in the United States, media auditing companies work for the advertiser to audit their media agencies and the media to provide a third-party verification of media plans and buys. These companies are the watchdogs for the advertisers in an ever-more-complicated landscape of media measurement.

Media accountability used to be confined to media delivery issues. The next stage of media accountability is on the actual effect of the schedule in the marketplace.

Tracking the impact of advertising has always been shrouded in mystery. Many say that there are too many factors that go into a purchase to "tease out" or isolate the impact of advertising. Others maintain that advertising is not always designed to stimulate sales now but is intended to put a consumer in the consideration set.

However, two key developments have made media accountability in terms of effect more readily available than it was in the past. The first is the growing sophistication of marketers using consumer database information to understand how and why consumers buy their brands. The second is the rise of the Internet as a crucial marketing tool.

There have always been ways of tracking the effectiveness of advertising media. For example, if an advertisement in 40 newspapers includes a cents-off coupon, counting the number of coupons redeemed from each source can help with estimates of how each newspaper did in getting the coupons into the hands of customers. Retailers and manufacturers have been doing this type of analysis for years.

The difference now is that most retailers have sophisticated point-of-sale (POS) information that is linked to databases that can be used for ongoing analysis. Most consumer packaged-goods (CPG) marketers use some form of marketing-mix analysis to isolate the importance of advertising, consumer promotion, and trade promotion on the impact of their business. As data have become more robust, CPG marketers have relied on statistical modeling to provide historical details on media spending and media vehicle contribution to sales. Many top CPG manufacturers, such as Procter & Gamble, now use market simulation data to forecast the future impact of varying media schedules and marketing mixes. While this type of analysis is more common among packaged-goods manufacturers, retailers and even business-to-business marketers are applying more high-level statistical analyses to their advertising effects in an effort to better understand performance of message and media strategies.

The second huge impact in the area of accountability is the rise of the Internet. One key reason for the popularity of Internet advertising is that the click-through rate (that is, how many advertising site visitors continue to another related Web site with more detailed information) can be tracked. Any direct orders that come from the Internet site can obviously be traced back to the actual Web page—in addition to possibly gaining some information about the customers and the opportunity to build up a continuing relationship with the customers who visit the Web site.

The Internet has the combination of direct-response accountability along with the impact of consumer-driven media such as television. Internet advertising schedules allow an advertiser to understand what creative and what media combinations are working the best on an ongoing basis. This benefit is a huge attraction to advertisers who previously had to wait for as long as a year to understand whether their television or magazine schedules were producing results. Advertisers who review cost-per-click or cost-per-sale data can immediately tell their management how their schedules are performing. Even advertisers who are using the Internet for a branding campaign can use tools such as Millward Brown's Dynamic Logic to track consumer attitudes toward the advertiser on an ongoing basis. The immediate and detailed accountability of the Internet is putting pressure on other media and agencies to be more accountable for their advertising.

Although there are still considerable challenges in linking cause and effect of sales to advertising, marketers and their agencies are becoming increasingly more sophisticated in their approach to solving this age-old dilemma. Many marketers are now challenging their agencies to put all or part of their compensation on the line based on some form of measured accountability. Sometimes this measure is sales, sometimes it is traffic counts, and other times it is a form of attitudinal changes. Regardless of the measure, media accountability is at the forefront of most marketers' minds.

Tools and Techniques

New tools and techniques help make such effectiveness tracing more feasible, as well as speeding up the advertising media planning and buying processes. The computer, for example, is now the primary tool in the advertising media business.

The computer can save and present millions of bits of information, data that once were available only in large books of research findings. The computer can store the information in its own memory or on CD-ROMs or DVDs, or the information can be accessed through the computer by tapping into a giant online database of research and related information.

The computer can also speed up the trial-and-error process of testing various combinations of media. Because the computer can make its calculations so rapidly, it can test several plans against one another in what is known as an iterative process; that is, it can be done over and over again very rapidly until the closest possible match is found.

As we mentioned earlier, computer databases are a key tool in nearly every media analysis in today's media agency. One problem with databases has been that consumer behavior data and media audience data were separate and couldn't be linked together. However, a new technique called data fusion has allowed media agencies to ascribe consumer behavior databases with media audience data. Because most consumer behavior data have common elements such as zip codes or even name-and-address data, there is an opportunity to fuse or link multiple databases together to leverage learning across a variety of platforms.

While marketing mix modeling (MMA) is still primarily confined to large consumer packaged-goods manufacturers, advertising industry software companies such as Telmar and IMS now offer "canned" marketing-mix models to help media professionals allocate their funds effectively. Media planners plug in their data from past years so that they can evaluate media schedules in terms of sales response functions.

Other statistical analysis such as CHAID (Chi-square Automatic Interaction Detector) is now being more widely used to determine the optimum target market for a brand. CHAID isolates demographic variables on how likely they are to be brand responders, and then develops a decision-tree style report so that the media planner can prioritize various target audience variables.

In addition, a number of media software and research companies are tackling the issue of channel media planning. Channel planning is a look at all the touchpoints of the consumer purchase process that go well beyond the traditional media set. This information may include friends and family advice, point of sale, collateral material, or any type of item that might influence the purchase of the brand. Channel planning software is based on consumers' ratings of the brands they purchase in categories such as trust, price, quality, and dependability. Then, consumers rate every media touchpoint on these same dimensions, and the software begins to correlate the two.

Channel planning is one analytical method that is growing in the media community. This process is determining how media fit into the context of the brand and the consumer's life, and its use has led to a rise in qualitative measurement and account planners "weighing in" on media choices. Once the province of media metrics, channel planning has taken on a combination of quantitative and qualitative dimensions.

With the continued pace of information and the ability of computers to synthesize data, the media tools of today are constantly evolving.

Future Trends

The advertising business is changing rapidly, and new media are constantly being developed. What you can be certain of is that you will work in a changing media environment. The media agency is changing rapidly as well. The media function was once a simple process of efficiency analysis for predetermined media mixes that were dictated by the creative department. Today, media agencies are providing counsel on not only media efficiency and effectiveness but on consumer behavior trends and how they impact advertising and media choices, as well as on marketing issues such as return on investment analysis. The media departments of the future are a combination of both high-level quantitative and qualitative thinking. The trends in the future mirror the changes of the media viewpoint.

We see five overall trends unfolding within the next few years. These trends are convergence, interactivity, engagement, commoditization, and cadence.

Convergent media are very important trends. The media are becoming more alike in many ways and are working together in new combinations. For example, even though newspaper circulations are declining, the use of Internet Web sites to access newspaper content is growing. The combination of newspapers and Internet is, thus, an example of media convergence. Other examples of convergent media are providing television programs over the Internet or through an iPod, magazines sponsoring special events for subscribers, television stations transmitting radio programming on a special weather channel, and outdoor signs carrying portions of television commercials.

Convergence also involves the similar formats used by many media, in which the news, information, features, and advertising signals are digitized and transmitted electronically from one location to another.

There are many implications of convergence. One is that advertising media professionals may have to evaluate and purchase content across a variety of platforms versus the traditional method of purchasing one media at a time. Reach and frequency measures that have been largely medium-by-medium based will have to be enhanced to allow media professionals to quickly assess the growing array of choices in the media landscape.

Exhibit 17.1

*Five Trends in Media Are Driving Change in the Media
Environment and Structure*

Robert G. Picard

Abundance, audience fragmentation and polarization, portfolio development, eroding strength of media firms, and a power shift in communications relationships are fundamentally reshaping the media marketplace as we know it.

Underlying the changes is a dramatic increase in the types of media and media units, creating media supply that far exceeds the growth in demand.

That abundance means that audiences are spreading their use across more media and media units. This produces extremes of use and non-use of channels and titles. Those choices are being mirrored by advertisers who are spreading their expenditures but are demanding to pay less for the smaller audiences.

Media companies have responded to declining profits per unit created by the audience and advertiser changes by developing portfolios of products in hopes of maintaining overall profits through more efficient operations and joint cost savings. Despite the portfolio developments, media companies are more unstable today than in previous decades because their reach has declined and they are financially weaker.

This weakness is reflected in the facts that major media companies today are concerned that they may be takeover targets and are regularly struggling with their major investors over strategy and performance.

The media communication process is undergoing a transformation from the days when the process was controlled by media companies to a situation in which it is increasingly controlled by consumers.

This shift from a supply market to a demand market is making consumers far more important than in the past. Today, for every dollar that advertisers put into media, consumers are spending three, so media must increasingly focus on creating value for them.

Dr. Robert G. Picard is Director of the Media Management and Transformation Centre, Jönköping International Business School, Sweden. Used by permission.

Many aspects of convergent media involve the Internet and other uses of personal computers, which permit *interactivity*. Advertisers have always wanted interactivity, such as sending along a pencil with a mailed magazine renewal notice, so the subscriber would act on the offer immediately. Now, with the Internet, e-mail, and other computerized applications, it is possible to have immediate and extensive interactivity between individuals and between an advertiser and customer.

Interactivity is one form of *engagement*. Another attribute that is important to advertisers, engagement involves gaining the centered and focused attention of the potential customer, as well as working interactively. In recent years, engagement has become an important goal for advertising media, but it can be achieved through means other than computer applications. Shouting out the answers while viewing a television game show or telephoning in to vote for your favorite in a reality television show are also forms of engagement.

The Advertising Research Foundation (ARF) is taking engagement to a new level of media analysis. Studies have shown that the more engaged consumers are in a media vehicle, the more likely they are to remember and act upon the advertising. A new layer of media thought emerging from engagement seems to go against the historical media wisdom that a gross rating point (GRP) is a GRP. Engagement suggests a more qualitative viewpoint of media: it is much more rooted in the context of the message and medium within a consumer's life than with the simple act of getting a message in front of as many consumers as possible.

Commoditization is making items similar to one another so that they have the same attributes and appeal. All brands of aspirin are pretty much alike, and most advertising for pain relievers (known in the trade as analgesics) does not claim superiority but merely that "no other pain reliever is stronger." Most personal computers work in similar ways, most gasoline has the same octane and additives, and light bulbs come in standard wattages and lumens. Similarities among competitors makes the job of promoting one brand more difficult and the selection of advertising media more critical. If commoditization causes all local banks to offer the same services and to be open the same hours, then advertising must make those services appeal to consumers and match their needs and wants, and advertising media must reach the proper targets economically and effectively.

Cadence is the schedule and process of implementing a project, such as an advertising media campaign "buy." The order in which the steps are taken and the synchronization of the activities are the goal of cadence. It is not possible to buy advertising media time and space until the budget is secured, and the budget must match with the audience size and advertising weights desired. The cadence is critical to advertising media. It includes the pace and schedule for an advertising campaign, with the introductory, sustaining, and reminder phases all scheduled for maximized effect. With the frenzy of everyday life and the hectic nature of the advertising business, cadence will continue to grow in importance.

There will be new trends, to be sure, but again, it is important to remember that the fundamental traits, processes, measurements, and outcomes that we have discussed in this book will still be with us in the future. Perhaps they will appear in novel combinations and in newly developed media, but the basic advertising media objectives, strategies, and tactics will remain the same.

Appendix

How the Advertising Business Is Organized

Every business, including every advertising agency, has its own unique organization. It is simply not possible to discuss or demonstrate all the various organizational plans and schemes and designs that are used in advertising.

Still, understanding how the media operations in advertising fit in with the overall advertising operations will help you comprehend how the business functions and how the media operations mesh with the rest of the advertising work.

In advertising agencies, there are two major themes used in agency organization. In the *departmental organization,* the various advertising functions are grouped together in departments. The advertising work flows go from one department to the next: from research to media and copywriting and art, all controlled though account services by the account executive or account supervisor. Exhibit A.2 shows a common type of departmental arrangement. However, as stated before, each agency is different, so no two organizational charts will be exactly alike.

Each department is composed of specialists in given activities who work on a variety of accounts. The work is spread out to keep the pace more even. Thus, the media department can handle the media planning, estimating, buying, and checking for all of the advertiser clients, moving from one account to another as necessary.

In an *account team organization,* the agency is organized into small teams, almost like small agencies within the bigger agency. Each account team has a mix of specialists who work on their own parts of the advertising campaign, and the entire team handles one or a few advertiser accounts. The entire list of accounts is split up among the various account teams, each team working on only a few of the accounts. In Exhibit A.3, a sample of the account teams' organization is diagrammed, but the actual composition of an account team might be

Exhibit A.1

Organizational Charts

Large organizations draw charts to show how they are organized. These organizational charts indicate levels of authority, lines of communication and control, and names and job titles or descriptions.

   The higher a position is on an organizational chart, the more important it is. People in top spots have more authority over personnel and decision making for their firm. (See the organizational chart.) Thus, the board chairperson or president is typically at the top of the organizational chart, and the middle and lower management positions are farther down.

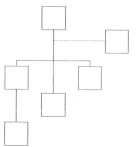

   On the organizational chart, positions are joined by lines that are either solid or dotted. Solid lines indicate both communication and control, and they are thus called line positions. Dotted lines indicate staff positions, meaning that communication exists but control does not. Line positions, then, have a say in how things are done, as well as the ability to communicate with those connected by organizational lines, whereas staff positions are usually advisory in nature, and although they still have communication with those connected by dotted lines, staff positions do not have a say in how things are done.

   Generally, formal communication between two distant persons on the chart just goes through the intermediaries—that is, through the positions intercepted by the lines joining the two original individuals. In practice, of course, people can send e-mail messages and make telephone calls to most of the others in the organization, but formal requests and approvals go through the other positions that come between them along the lines that connect them.

   Individual boxes usually indicate certain positions, including both the job title and the name of the person currently filling that position.

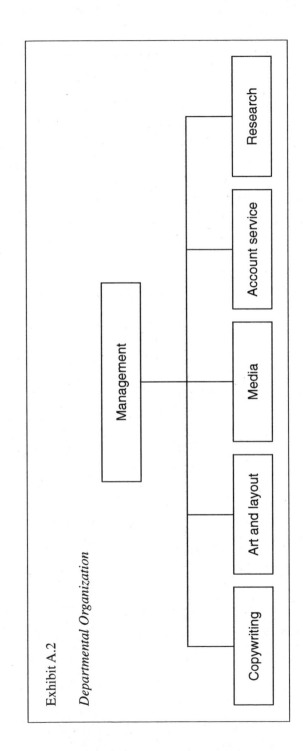

Exhibit A.2

Departmental Organization

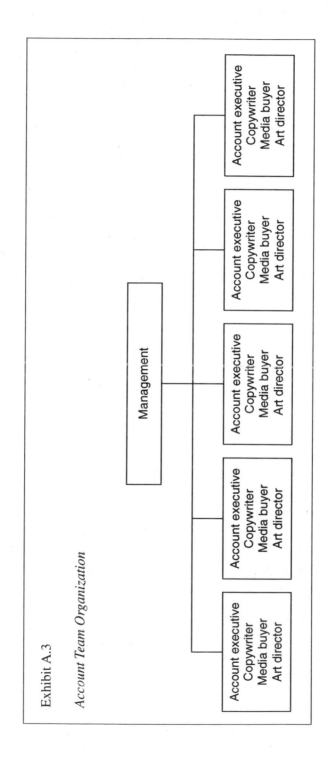

Exhibit A.3

Account Team Organization

larger or smaller; the diagram shows only one possible type of team specialty combination.

The advantage of the account team setup is that the teams become accustomed to working together and know their own accounts quite well. The disadvantages include getting stale from working on the same account all the time, as well as some periods of time with high workloads and others with low workloads. The advertising media personnel may handle the entire load without much contact with other media staffers.

A small advertising agency may be organized in a manner similar to that shown in Exhibit A.3, but with a few differences. An organizational chart from an actual advertising agency, using the account team plan, is shown in Exhibit A.4.

A larger advertising agency will, of course, be more complex. Exhibit A.5 shows a medium-sized advertising agency with a departmental arrangement. Note that this is not the entire organizational chart for the agency, only the media department's organization.

Very large advertising agencies will be even more complex. A large advertising agency will have many more specializations and, consequently, many more specialists. Only the media department of a large advertising agency is shown in Exhibit A.6.

Advertisers—the clients of advertising agencies—are organized quite differently. They do not need media estimators, media planners, or media buyers because that work is normally handled at the agency, not at the advertiser (client) company.

A small national company's advertising department is portrayed in Exhibit A.7. Note that even though the titles deal with advertising, the emphasis appears to be on marketing in general. The media portion of the client company's advertising effort is handled primarily by the media director, who oversees the agency's work and serves as the direct liaison between the advertiser and the agency.

A large firm will have a more complex advertising department. In Exhibit A.8, the advertising operations of a large industrial company are displayed as an entire division of the corporation. This division works on a variety of media efforts unique to the corporation and its industry, which requires multiple departments and staff. Even though an advertising agency handles media estimating, planning, and buying, there is still a lot of detailed media work done by this advertiser's media department.

Although each of the organizational charts displayed here is unique to an individual firm, together they should provide you with a solid overview of the types of organizations used to manage and control advertising media operations in a variety of firms and settings.

172

Exhibit A.4

Small Advertising Agency

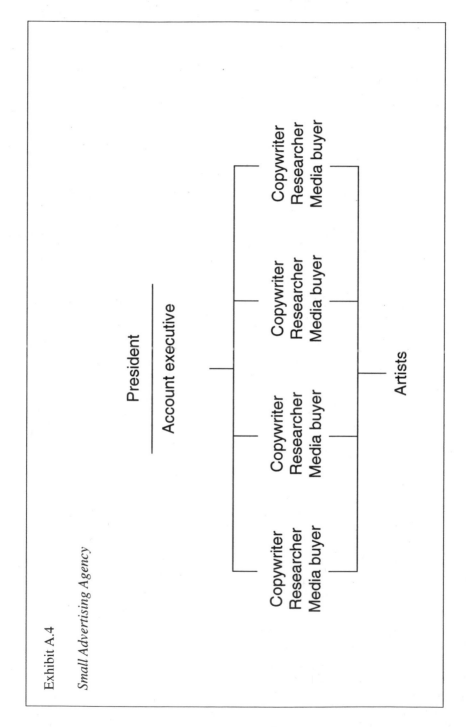

President

Account executive

Copywriter
Researcher
Media buyer

Copywriter
Researcher
Media buyer

Copywriter
Researcher
Media buyer

Copywriter
Researcher
Media buyer

Artists

Exhibit A.5

Medium Advertising Agency

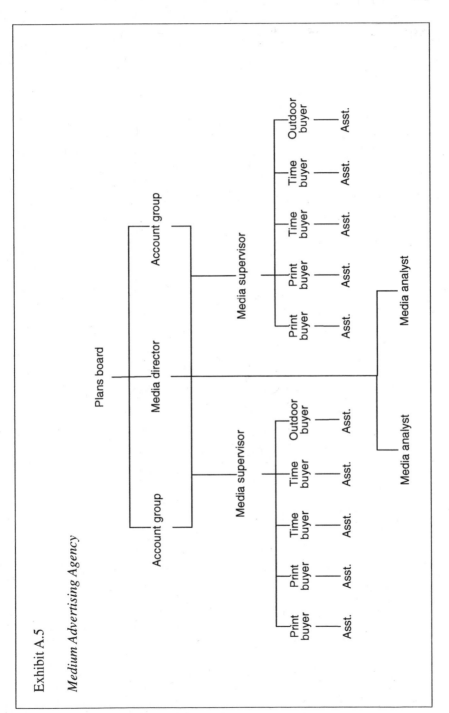

Exhibit A.6

Large Advertising Agency

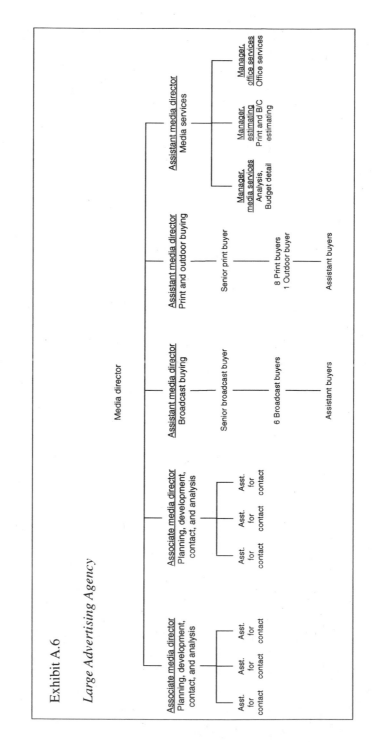

175

Exhibit A.7

Advertising Department, Smaller Company

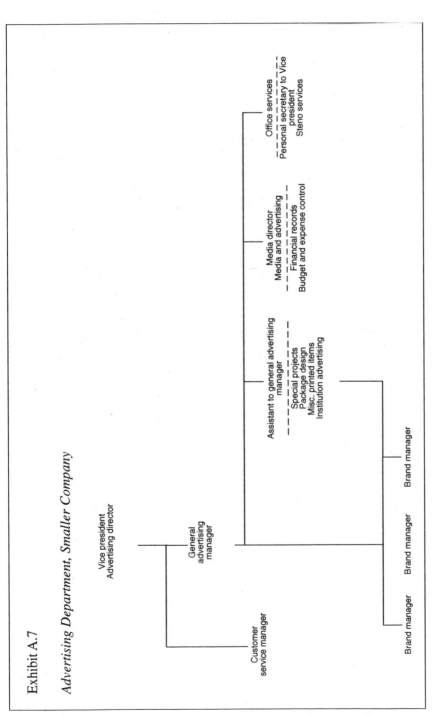

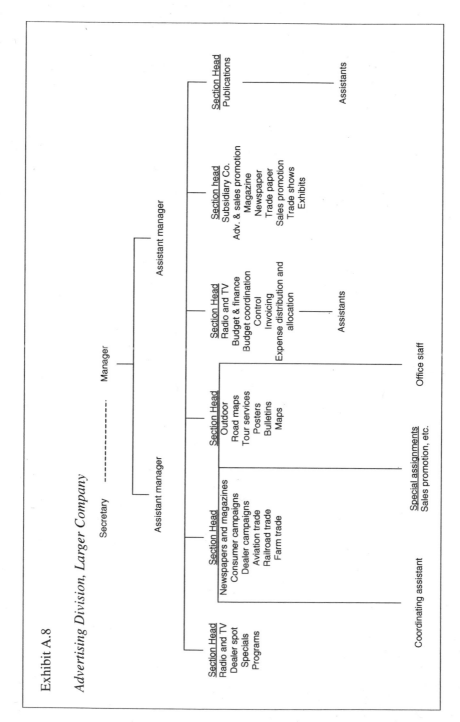

Exhibit A.8

Advertising Division, Larger Company

Index

Boldface page references indicate exhibits and tables.

About the Authors

Larry D. Kelley is an executive vice president with FKM advertising agency, where he is responsible for the planning arm of the agency called the Targeting Group. He is also a clinical professor at the University of Houston.

Mr. Kelley began his career in Dallas at the Bloom Agency, becoming manager of media research within his first two years at the agency. He held senior management positions that encompassed media and research at Bozell & Jacobs and at Batten, Barton, Durstine, and Osborn Advertising Agency (BBDO) before joining FKM in 1990. Since that time, he has helped lead strategy on such accounts as ConAgra Foods, Daisy Sour Cream, Riviana Foods, Advance Auto Parts, Conoco, Waste Management, and Dell computer company.

Mr. Kelley is widely quoted in trade publications such as *Adweek* and *Advertising Age*. He is the coauthor of *Advertising Media Planning: A Brand Management Approach* and *Advertising Media Workbook and Sourcebook* with Dr. Donald W. Jugenheimer. He is also the author of an industry book on account planning published by the American Association of Advertising Agencies (4As), the trade association for the advertising community.

Mr. Kelley is on the board of directors for the Retail Marketing Institute, the Advisory Council for Radio Measurement, and the 4A's Media Council. He has a B.S. in journalism from the University of Kansas and a master's degree from the University of Texas at Austin.

Dr. Donald W. Jugenheimer is professor of advertising and chair of the Department of Advertising at Texas Tech University. His teaching specialties are media management, media economics, and advertising media.

Since earning his Ph.D. in communications from the University of Illinois at Urbana-Champaign with a specialization in advertising and a minor in marketing, Dr. Jugenheimer has been a tenured member of the faculties at the University of Kansas, Louisiana State University (where he was the first person to hold the Manship Distinguished Professorship in Journalism),

Fairleigh Dickinson University, and Southern Illinois University. He holds a bachelor's degree in advertising with a minor in economics and a master's degree in advertising with a minor in marketing, also from the University of Illinois.

Dr. Jugenheimer is author or coauthor of 15 books and many articles and papers. He has spoken before a variety of academic and professional organizations. He also served as president and executive director of the American Academy of Advertising, and as advertising division head of the Association for Education in Journalism and Mass Communication. In addition, he was business manager for the founding of the *Journal of Advertising.*

As a consultant, Dr. Jugenheimer has worked with such firms as American Airlines, IBM, Century 21 Real Estate, Aetna Insurance, Pacific Telesis, and the U.S. Army Recruiting Command. He has also conducted research for a variety of enterprises, including the U.S. Department of Health, Education and Welfare, the International Association of Business Communicators, and National Liberty Life Insurance. He has lectured and conducted workshops in several countries and is a guest faculty member of the Executive Media MBA program for the Turku School of Economics and Business Administration in Finland. A recipient of the Kellogg National Fellowship, Dr. Jugenheimer is listed in *Who's Who in America, Who's Who in Advertising, Who's Who in Education,* and several other biographical references.